Digital Visual Literacy

DIGITAL VISUAL LITERACY

The Librarian's Quick Guide

Nicole M. Fox

LIBRARIES
UNLIMITED®
An Imprint of ABC-CLIO, LLC
Santa Barbara, California • Denver, Colorado

Library of Congress Cataloging-in-Publication Data

Names: Fox, Nicole M., author.
Title: Digital visual literacy : the librarian's quick guide / Nicole M. Fox.
Description: Santa Barbara, California : Libraries Unlimited, 2022. |
    Includes bibliographical references and index.
Identifiers: LCCN 2021055615 (print) | LCCN 2021055616 (ebook) |
    ISBN 9781440875175 (paperback) | ISBN 9781440875182 (ebook)
Subjects: LCSH: Visual literacy. | Computer literacy. | Digital humanities.
Classification: LCC LB1068 .F68 2022 (print) | LCC LB1068 (ebook) |
    DDC 371.33/5—dc23/eng/20211213
LC record available at https://lccn.loc.gov/2021055615
LC ebook record available at https://lccn.loc.gov/2021055616

ISBN: 978-1-4408-7517-5 (paperback)
       978-1-4408-7518-2 (ebook)

26 25 24 23 22   1 2 3 4 5

This book is also available as an eBook.

Libraries Unlimited
An Imprint of ABC-CLIO, LLC

ABC-CLIO, LLC
147 Castilian Drive
Santa Barbara, California 93117
www.abc-clio.com

This book is printed on acid-free paper ∞

Manufactured in the United States of America

To my wonderful husband, Santhanai,
for always believing in me. You're the best!

And to Claire and Jenny, the best instruction librarians
I've ever met! Thank you for supporting and
guiding me as a librarian.

Contents

What Is Visual Literacy?

As librarians, we get the pleasure of working with and sharing a variety of different information sources, from traditional books and articles to preserved ephemera in special collections. Libraries have been quick to adapt over the years, embracing new forms of born-digital information. However, much like in other areas in academia, there remains a reluctance to see images for what they really are: not just decorative art, but valuable sources of information. Today, the vast majority of images we encounter on a daily basis have touched the internet in one form or another, whether they were created digitally through the use of tools like Photoshop, digitized and stored in a library's online repository, or shared on social media. People say that a picture is worth a thousand words—but images are much more than the many thousands of words you could use in their description. It's perhaps better to measure a picture by the forms, elements, contexts, and meanings that make up each one of the images we encounter on a daily basis.

This book is designed to be a quick, informative guide to visual literacy instruction in any classroom, not just the art or design classroom. In order to connect visual literacy instruction to the digital space it now occupies, this book also features several workshops and instruction sessions that use digital humanities tools. Maybe you've struggled with finding an innovative way to keep your students engaged in an image copyright one-shot lesson or you need to find a great image evaluation workshop suitable for use in an online course; either way, this book should serve as a useful resource in your instruction planning.

INTRODUCTION TO DIGITAL VISUAL LITERACY

Whenever I talk to a fellow librarian about visual literacy, the most common question I get is: What exactly *is* visual literacy, anyways? How does it differ from information literacy? While visual literacy has become somewhat of a buzzword, it's not a major part of MLS curriculums, and it remains jargon to most teaching librarians outside of the arts—much less to students.

Understanding Visual Literacy

Simply put, visual literacy is the ability to construct meaning from images.[1] When you look at a picture, you see it for what it is at its most basic level, which is usually a visual representation of a physical object. For example, take a look at Photo 1.1.

We can derive meaning from it just by giving it a cursory glance. From a basic examination of this image, we can tell it's a picture of a barren, rocky landscape with a dark sky. The picture itself is not entirely impressive. There's nothing colorful, unexpected, or interesting that catches the viewer's eye, and it's grainy and marred with lighter stripes.

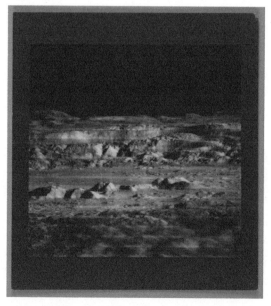

PHOTO 1.1. Close-Up of Crater Copernicus. November 23, 1966, National Aeronautics and Space Administration.
Source: NASA.

But there's more that gives an image meaning than just the actual picture itself. Take a look at the image caption. The title, date, and credit add valuable context to this picture. This isn't just a picture of a desolate landscape, it's a photo taken on the *moon*. This context transforms this image from bland to something quite extraordinary. The landscape somehow becomes even more barren, now that we know there's no life hidden among the rocks and ridges in the picture. Though it's grainy compared to the high-resolution images we're accustomed to, it marks the very height of technological advances during the time in which it was taken. It's easy enough to derive meaning from images, but visual literacy as a concept is more focused on navigating the many different layers of meaning that are attached to each image.

Let's look again at our moon photo. If this photo were being used to illustrate a narrative describing the moon, the viewer would need to decipher *why* this photo, over the millions of other photos of the moon, was selected. Usually pictures emphasize the narratives they illustrate; they're a conscious choice made by a creator. If this photo accompanied an article that described the moon as totally unsuitable for any future colonization efforts a country might attempt, this photo would echo and amplify those ideas. The moon here appears bleak and unfriendly, and the photo emphasizes the idea that it's an unsuitable landscape for human life. This is due, in part, to the use of artistic principles in the image. In our example, the use of color makes this photo appear lifeless and almost foreboding—the landscape is mostly dark, and the sky above the crater is an endless black, unbroken by any celestial objects. If a writer wanted to say the opposite—that is, that with the right tools a colony could flourish on the moon, they would certainly not select this image to accompany their article. A photo such as the famous *Earthrise* from NASA could be a better choice. With our planet rising in the lunar sky, this image makes the moon feel not quite so far from home. Though the sky is just as dark, there are also a lot of lighter colors in this image, which ultimately serves to emphasize the lighter lunar surface and the gleaming Earth. Even a photo of a full moon hanging in the night sky as a source of light in the middle of the night would look more inviting and optimistic. This intent in image selection is yet another meaning-layer that can be interpreted from visual materials, and any visually literate viewer should try to determine what kind of story the image is trying to tell the viewer.

The visually literate individual doesn't just investigate what an image depicts or why an image is used, however, particularly when using images for their projects. Knowing the copyright and other ethical considerations is yet another type of meaning-layer that needs to be navigated when using images. Though it's easy to find images, not everyone gives credit for the images they use in their assignments, nor does everyone know what images can be used for what purpose. Much like how an information literate writer knows how to cite the works they use, the same must be done for any images that the user hasn't personally created. There are many types of licenses and policies that can also affect an image's ability to be used for a project. Understanding the public domain, fair use, and Creative Commons licenses will give students and other users the freedom to use and create different kinds of image-rich projects, as well as share them with the world. *Close-Up of Crater Copernicus*, our first example image, is in the public domain and is available through the Metropolitan Museum of Art's Open Access Policy, and the title, date, and organization are cited in the image's caption. The visually literate viewer could take that caption information and not just use it to provide context about the image; they could use it to find out more about where the image was originally found.

Visual Literacy Standards

With a concept as complex as visual literacy, librarians will need tools to scaffold the larger idea into manageable principles. One tool that's particularly helpful in understanding the intricacies of visual literacy are the ACRL Visual Literacy Standards for Higher Education. These standards can function as a framework for both understanding and teaching the many different aspects of visual literacy. If you're teaching in another setting, the rigor of these standards can also be scaled to suit a variety of classrooms. The standards define visual literacy as a set of seven core skills that allow a student to both use and create images and other visual sources effectively in undergraduate college work. Each of these core skills, or standards, is mapped to a series of performance indicators and learning outcomes.[2] When designing your visual literacy curriculum, these learning outcomes can be a great way to measure the success of your instruction and to tie into other aspects of your student learning outcomes. The different aspects of both visual literacy and the ACRL framework can be divided into four main overarching frameworks: **finding images, evaluating images, communicating with images,** and **ethical use of images**.

In order to **find the images** that students need for their research projects and other assignments, students need to be able to articulate their image needs and understand the characteristics of different kinds of images—particularly digital images. Then, students need to be equipped with the tools and strategies to conduct effective image searches. **Image evaluation** is a crucial skill in understanding not just who created the image but also what kind of story the artist or photographer was trying to tell. Students should not only be able to evaluate the image source, context associated with the image, and accompanying metadata but also use traditional design knowledge and art vocabulary to interpret their deeper, and sometimes hidden, meanings. Students who effectively **communicate with images** need to be able to use tools to edit and create images. Students need to do more than just design images, however; they need to be able to evaluate and critique their own work. Finally, there's a variety of **copyright and ethical considerations** in using images. Image citation, attribution, and captions are complicated, murky worlds. Librarians need to feel equipped in handling these ethical issues, because there's minimal guidance from the style handbooks themselves. The same can be said of the legal intricacies of image use. Copyright and fair use are not always easy or fun concepts to discuss with students, but they're important and even essential skills in our digital, visual world.

Teaching Visual Literacy—Digitally

If visual literacy is understanding the many layers of meanings associated with visual media, then what's digital visual literacy? How is digital visual literacy different from "regular" visual literacy? Why should instructors consider visual literacy as a form of digital knowledge?

Traditionally, visual literacy has been considered part of the art and design curriculum. This may have made sense when visual materials were mostly relegated to the realm of the arts. After all, it was only a few decades ago that in order to create images, you needed to have some sort of basic artistic skill or access to specialized, and often expensive, equipment like cameras. But digital technologies have changed our relationship to visual media access. Today, *anyone* can create pictures. An estimated 1.2 trillion digital photos were taken in 2017,[3] a figure that has only grown as more and more people gain access to smartphones and the internet. In addition, students in all kinds of programs are being asked to create images as a regular part of their coursework. Statistics and math students make graphs and other charts; students in the sciences document the natural world and how it changes. History students use images of primary sources in their assignments. Students of all disciplines create presentations illustrated with stock photos and design blogs. Image creation is now a huge part of our daily lives and academic landscapes.

In the digital age, it's not just a matter of being able to create images more easily. Students simply have access to more images as well. Google Image Search has revolutionized the way we search for images. Finding just about any picture you can dream of is as easy as entering some keywords into a search bar. Because of these advances in digital technologies, it's important to realize that visual literacy is no longer confined to the arts. Visual literacy, or the lack thereof, is now every librarian's issue.

Because so many pictures are now freely available and easily accessible, and so many students are now engaged in image creation, it's important to reframe visual literacy as a broader issue. If we, as librarians and teachers, keep thinking of visual literacy as a skill set best left for those in the arts, we're doing our students a disservice. That's why this book is framing visual literacy as *digital* visual literacy. We've already discussed what visual literacy means, so let's have a brief overview of digital literacy in order to better understand where visual literacy fits under the digital literacies umbrella. Literacy is a word that keeps appearing in the library world, often accompanied by other words like "information" or "visual." The most basic meaning of the word "literacy" means "the ability to read and write." But literacy means something more than just the ability to read and write, especially when used in a phrase like *visual literacy*. It also means you're able to participate in something important, something that's a normal part of our everyday culture.

Digital literacy, then, if we look at our previous definition of the word "literacy," refers to the skills needed to successfully and safely navigate the digital world. Digital literacy, for example, is knowing how to navigate to a website in an internet browser. The digitally literate student knows how to format a uniform resource locator (URL) and where to type that URL in. However, what about using the website itself? Evaluating a website for reliability and relevance is a skill that we librarians consider to be part of information literacy, but it's certainly linked to digital literacy. The boundaries between digital literacy and other forms of literacy have become indistinct as more and more information is accessed online. As our understanding of digital technologies has changed, so, too, has our understanding of digital literacy. There's not just one set of skills that a student needs in order to successfully navigate the digital world.

Visual literacy is similar to information in that it's now a skill set that's linked to digital literacy. Students may know how to save images they find on the internet, but do they know how to select the best format for their project or properly cite an image they found using Google Image Search? By packaging visual literacy under the digital umbrella, we, as instructors, can more easily apply the skills of visual literacy to the variety of situations in which students encounter images today.

USING THIS BOOK

This book is intended to be a quick guide to teaching digital visual literacy in higher education. Each chapter discusses a different facet of visual literacy through a digital lens. In Chapter 2: Identifying and Finding Images, I introduce digital image types and discuss the basics of online image searching, including using databases and other resources. In Chapter 3: Evaluating and Interpreting Images, I cover different considerations for judging image reliability in an online environment, vocabulary for describing images, and image context. Chapter 4: Designing and Communicating with Images covers how to teach image creation and modification in a library instruction session, the power of images as a storytelling tool, and how to help your students learn to evaluate their own visual creations. Chapter 5: Citation and Ethics for Images discusses image citation and other legal issues that relate to image use, like public domain, fair use, and Creative Commons. In Chapter 6: Activities and Assignments, I share six different digital-based activities you can use to teach visual literacy to your students, whether it's in a long-term course or a one-shot library instruction session. Finally, in Chapter 7: Conclusion, I help you prepare for the ever-changing future of digital visual literacy by discussing future considerations in visual literacy studies.

NOTES

1. Giorgis, Cyndi, Nancy J. Johnson, Annamarie Bonomo, Chrissie Colbert, Angela Conner, Gloria Kauffman, and Dottie Kulesza. "Children's Books: Visual Literacy." *The Reading Teacher* 53, no. 2 (1999): 146–53.
2. "ACRL Visual Literacy Competency Standards for Higher Education." Association of College & Research Libraries (ACRL), October 27, 2011. http://www.ala.org/acrl/standards/visualliteracy.
3. Richter, Felix. "Infographic: Smartphones Cause Photography Boom." Statista Infographics, August 31, 2017. https://www.statista.com/chart /10913/number-of-photos-taken-worldwide.

2

Identifying and Finding Images

The visually literate student should be able to identify and find a variety of images. This is because different projects and assignments will need different kinds of images. Finding the right image is a process that takes some careful consideration on the part of the searcher. It's important to take a moment to ask yourself a series of questions about the image you're looking for, as this will allow you to express exactly what you're looking for more clearly. This chapter will start with going over how to lead your students through the process of identifying their image needs. Once your students have a clear idea about what images they need for their research, it's time to start searching the Web—a daunting task, considering you'll need to sift through literally billions of images. Knowing where to start your search—whether it's in an image database, a digital repository, or through the use of Google Image Search—can help you narrow down your search, as well as begin crafting an appropriate search strategy.

Finally, we'll cover how to organize all this visual information. Just like with other types of information, students need to be able to provide their sources in order to share them and properly cite them. Properly organizing your visual information can also allow your students to spot patterns and see similarities in a series of images—which could spark some new ideas or thoughts.

TYPES OF IMAGES

Knowing the purpose of your image will help your students determine what kind of images they should search for. In order to find the most suitable picture for their project, students should ask themselves some questions before they get started with searching. Knowing why you're using an image, who your audience is, and how you're going to use the image will allow for more effective searching.

Crafting a Narrative

The first question a student should ask is **why** am I using an image? There are a lot of different kinds of images out there, and understanding why you're using an image will help you decide what serves your project best, as well as where you begin searching. Are you, for example, trying to use an image as evidence of a main point in a research paper? Or are you using an image to illustrate a slide on a presentation? Both of these uses would require different images—even if they were about the same topic. There's an almost infinite variety of ways you could categorize images. People tend to categorize images by medium, or what was used to create the picture. People also categorize images by subject matter—what the image itself pictures. However, these categories aren't as helpful to the student researcher, who needs to not just view a picture but *use* an image in their work. Instead of categorizing images by how they're created or by what their subject matter is, you should consider categorizing images by their potential use in your project.

While there's a lot of different kinds of images out there, most of them can be categorized into one of three groups: known images, illustrative images, and visualizations. These categories refer not to how the image is created, but instead what purpose it's being used for. An illustrative image, for example, doesn't have to be a drawing—it could be a photograph. **Known images** are images of specific persons, places, or things. Known images sometimes serve as a primary source in a research project; other times they simply illuminate the content to the viewer. Take this image of Edgar Allan Poe (Photo 2.1), for example.

If you were presenting on different kinds of engraving techniques, this might be a good known image. It could function as a primary source, visibly demonstrating a certain engraving technique. If you were a student writing a research paper on the public acclaim of Edgar Allan Poe, this image could also function as a known image. If the reader was unfamiliar with Poe, this could help "picture" the topic. **Illustrative images** are images used to illustrate concepts. They function symbolically rather than literally. Illustrative pictures are sometimes used to clarify a vaguer concept than a person, place, or thing—perhaps a feeling or a philosophical ideal. Stock images, which are nonspecific professional photos usually made for graphic designers, often function as illustrative images. An image of an open window is an example of an illustrative image. It's not an image of a specific place or time—it's just an open window. However, it could be used to help the audience understand a certain concept. If a student were presenting on the importance of maintaining an open mind in education, this image would be suitable. **Visualizations** are images of a specific set of data. Charts and graphs are common forms of visualizations. People don't often think of visualizations as images, but they need to be created and evaluated much like other images are, even though they often contain words or numbers.

PHOTO 2.1. Portrait of Edgar Allan Poe (from *Scribner's Monthly Magazine*). 1880. Engraved by Timothy Cole.
Source: Gift of Mrs. Alfred G. Mayer, 1933. Courtesy of the Metropolitan Museum of Art.

As these categories are based on image use, the same image can shift from one category to another based on what kind of project. Take, for example, this image (Photo 2.2) of women studying.

Depending on how you use this image, it could be either a known image or an illustrative image. If a student were writing a blog post about the history of women's education, this could be a suitable illustrative image. It shows an example of women studying in a historical setting, without it being about a specific person or place. It could help illustrate to the readers how women's education used to function.

This is an image from Belmont University's digital repository, and if we read about the origins of the image, the student could use it in a different manner. If a student were researching about the history of women's education and how the role of women in education and as educators has changed over time, this could be a valuable known image. It could function as a primary source in such a project, as it shows women attending class at the Ward-Belmont School, a women's seminary in Nashville. Even though both of these example projects use a similar project and the exact same picture, what the picture adds to each project is different, because the student is using them for different purposes.

PHOTO 2.2. First-Rate Education. 1923. Belmont University Special Collections.
Source: Image used with permission from Belmont University.

So, why should you ask your students to think about the purpose of the image? Knowing why you're using an image will help you search for that image more effectively. It clarifies what you need and lets you formulate an appropriate search strategy. Brainstorming keywords for images varies by image use—see the "How to Search" section for more information.

Students should also consider their audience when selecting images for a project. Knowing **who** is going to be viewing this image will help them make better decisions. For example, a student presenting on the Civil War would probably want to include a map of certain battles mentioned in the main points of their argument. If the student is presenting to their classmates, their goal might be to instruct their fellow students on the topic. If that's the case, they'd need to select a map with some modern context. Choosing a map with clearly marked modern cities and state lines would help the less knowledgeable audience understand the image's content more easily. If they're presenting at an undergraduate conference or symposium, they'd consider perhaps choosing a very different map. In this situation, it's safe to assume that this audience would have some knowledge of the subject and so wouldn't need as much context. The student could search a digital repository and find a map of battles from that time period—an image that would be much more compelling to that audience.

Image File Formats

Next, the student should ask themselves **how** they are going to use an image. Is it going to be printed out on a poster or posted on a class blog? Knowing how an image will be used will allow them to select the appropriate image size and file type for the job.

There are dozens of file types out there, each with their own specific uses and strengths. Most of the time, students will be using one of these file types.

- **JPEG** is one of the most common digital image file types, and it stands for Joint Photographic Experts Group. JPEGs are also sometimes known as JPG. JPEGs can be used on the Web or for printing. The quality of a JPEG image is directly linked to its file size. So, if you edit or compress a JPEG image, you run the risk of affecting its quality.
- **PNG**, or Portable Network Graphics, is another common image file type used on the internet. PNGs *don't* lose quality when you edit them, and they can have a transparent background, making them a good choice for many web graphics. For highly detailed images, such as photographs, PNGs are often larger than the equivalent JPEG version for a similar level of quality.
- **GIF** images are usually animated. GIF stands for Graphic Interchange Format.
- **PDF**, or Portable Document Format, is thought of as a format for text documents. However, PDFs can also be used for images. PDFs are ideal for printing and for sharing with other people, but do not function well as web graphics.

Image quality is another important consideration. For digital images, image quality is usually referred to as **resolution**. The higher the resolution of an image, the more detail it has. Conversely, a low-resolution image has fewer details. Most image details can be measured by **pixels**. Pixels are the smallest visible elements in an image. If you zoom in on an image, you'll start to see individual squares or dots of colors—these are pixels. If an image has many pixels, it'll be more detailed, particularly if it's a larger size.

Resolution can be a confusing concept, because there are many different ways to measure resolution:

- **Pixel resolution** refers to the dimensions of pixels in an image and is usually expressed as horizontal × vertical. Common pixel resolutions are 640 × 480, 800 × 600, and 1024 × 768.
- **DPI** stands for "dots per inch" and measures how many actuals dots of ink a printer can print per inch.

- **PPI**, or pixels per inch, refers to how many pixels per inch are in a digital image. DPI and PPI are sometimes used interchangeably, but refer to slightly different measurements.

You can view an image's resolution by examining the details of the image. For PC users, after you download an image, right-click on it and select "Properties," and then click on the Details tab. You'll be able to see both the pixel resolution and the DPI. For Mac users, you can view the pixel resolution by control-clicking the image file in Finder, then clicking Get Info, and then selecting More Info.

How your students plan on using their images will determine the resolution needed for their project. Pixelated, low-resolution images don't get their point across in a presentation as well as high-quality, clear images. If students are printing out images, using a high-resolution image is very important. A large JPEG or a PDF might be a good choice. While high-resolution images seem like they'd be desirable for all uses, that's not always the case. An image that's too large might load very slowly on a website, making it less accessible.

IMAGE SEARCHING

Once a student has thought carefully about their image need and has answered the questions outlined earlier, they should have a clear idea of what they're actually looking for. Instead of just searching for a picture a student can use in a class blog post discussing the role of religion in British plays, you might actually be looking for a larger pixel resolution JPEG illustrative image of religion in drama that's also appropriate for the general public. So, now that you have some idea of what kind of image you need for your project, it's time to start your search. There are two main considerations in beginning an image search: where to search and how you search within your chosen source.

Where to Look

There's no shortage of great image repositories available on the internet. However, where should you get started? It can be overwhelming trying to select the right place to begin searching for your images. This section will provide a brief overview of common image resources, along with their benefits and drawbacks, so that you can best direct your students to the image resources they need. There are two main categories for digital image resources: databases and other web resources.

Databases

As a librarian, it's our nature to turn to library resources—like databases—when searching for an information need. Image databases, like ARTStor or Bridgeman, can be a great place to find a lot of images. Databases, with their metadata and smaller scope than that of the Web, can also be less overwhelming for students to explore and much easier to cite.

ARTstor is one of the more popular databases, and for good reason; with a subscription, you and your students have access to a diverse collection of over 2.5 million, high-quality images.[1] The Andrew W. Mellon Foundation started ARTstor in the 1990s, when universities and other academic institutions began the process of migrating their image collections from physical slides to digital images. ARTstor works with a variety of institutions and uses the metadata that's provided to them.[2]

While ARTstor has a strong collection of fine arts images, such as paintings and sculptures, it's also a great place to get some historical and popular culture images. Like other databases, ARTstor also has a series of powerful tools that allow you to both search for images and use them with ease. The Advanced Search function is specifically tailored for image searching, allowing you to search in fields like "material" and "style or period." If you'd prefer to browse images rather than use the search functions, the collections are set up in an easy-to-use manner. The classifications make sense for an image database and allow you to browse categories like "maps, charts, and graphs" and "fashion, costume, and jewelry." It also has a citation tool, much like other databases, allowing students to get a head start on formulating citations with the click of a button. Unfortunately, ARTstor isn't a free resource, and like most databases, a yearly subscription doesn't come cheaply. Plan to budget for this resource, should you decide to acquire it for your institution.

Bridgeman Education is another common image database. Unlike ARTstor, Bridgeman began not purely as a digital venture, but as the Bridgeman Art Library.[3] At 1.2 million images, Bridgeman has fewer images than ARTstor, but it's still a very useful collection.

Bridgeman has a number of other helpful database tools. One of Bridgeman's strengths is its metadata. This collection's strong metadata allows for ease of browsing—it feels very much like a digital museum, rather than just a database. There are some interesting collections to browse in the Subjects section of Bridgman, including Conceptual Images, which is a great source for illustrative images.

There are other, more specific, library database subscriptions that you can invest in, depending on what kind of programs your institution has. If your college has a fashion program or a strong interest in curating a popular culture collection, ProQuest's **Vogue Archive** is an incredible resource. The Vogue Archive is a digitized collection of every issue of American *Vogue*. It includes all of the images, ads, and text of each issue. The Image Details search function is a powerful tool that allows you to search not just by image-tailored fields like color and material. **Statista** is a powerful market data and statistics database. It has a wonderful Infographics section with many graphs, charts, and other kinds of visualizations. The **AP Newsroom** is a primary source database available from EBSCO that contains over 12 million images covering a variety of topics of both modern and historical significance.

Out on the Web

While databases are a great place to look for high-quality images, they're certainly not the only source of images on the internet. Out on the Web, you may find some wonderful image sources. You can start looking for internet image sources in one of two ways: you can utilize a search engine, or you can browse or search an individual website. For search engines, Google Image Search is the most popular choice for image searching, but it's not the only place you should look. Different search engines, of course, have different algorithms, so it's always a good idea to be flexible and be prepared to search in several different places.

Google Image Search

Google Image Search is a powerful image search engine. Most of the time, when confronted with the need to search for an image, it's the first place people turn to. Students are no exception to this, and with good reason. Google Image Search is easy and familiar to most searchers and allows you to search billions of images. Google Image Search has been helping users find the pictures they need since 2001, when searchers began looking for images of Jennifer Lopez's 2000 green Grammy Awards dress but were unable to do so. Today, students and other searchers can find almost any image they want just by entering keywords into Google Image's search bar.

If your students are comfortable with research techniques, you might want to direct them to Google's **Advanced Image Search** page, rather than the basic Google Image Search. This page, which can be found simply by searching for Google Advanced Image Search, allows searchers to craft a more complex search by using boolean-style logic. It also introduces the equivalent words and symbols for using this logic in a regular Google search, but the advanced search page is still useful as an introduction to the idea of creating complex image searches.

In addition, the Advanced Image Search page has powerful filter tools. These tools can also be used on a regular page of search results by clicking on the **Tools** link, underneath the search bar.

- The **Image size** filter lets the searcher filter their results by image resolution.
- The **Aspect ratio** filter allows the searcher to narrow their results by the shape of the image.

- The **Colors** filter lets users search for images that are a particular color. You can select one of 12 colors, or select full color, black and white, or transparent (which refers to the background of the image).

- The **Type** filter allows you to select an image from one of Google's predetermined categories: face, photo, clip art, line drawing, or animated.

- The **Region** filter allows you to select the country in which the picture was published.

- The **Site** filter allows you to search on a particular website for an image. This can be helpful for searching museum websites and other image-rich sites.

- The **SafeSearch** filter lets searchers filter out sexually explicit materials.

- The **File type** filter lets you search for a specific image file type, including some of the ones we covered earlier.

- The **Usage rights** filter lets you filter images by usage restrictions. Not all images have known restrictions, however, so sometimes this can needlessly limit results.

Bing Images

Some students may not even think to use an alternative image search engine, since Google use is so ingrained in our digital landscape. Even the act of using a search engine is no longer referred to as "searching," but instead as "Googling." Despite this, sometimes other search engines can offer different, and sometimes better, results. Bing is Microsoft's version of an internet search engine. Bing, while widely used, is not nearly as popular as Google. Bing Images functions much the same as Google Image Search; searchers simply enter in the keywords of their choosing into a search bar in order to get started.

The page of search results, at first glance, also looks very similar to Google Image Search. Results are displayed in a grid-like formation, and searchers must click on an individual image in order to see what webpage it comes from, as well as any other information the search engine could gather. Tools for filtering your search results are available at the top, just above the grid of results. These tools allow searchers to filter by size, type, and more, including license—which allows searchers to find images in the public domain or those with Creative Commons licenses.

The interface of an individual result is where it differs the most from Google Images. Google Image Search results take up about half the page and include the name of the website and a blurb from the page. There's also a section of related images—visually similar images that could be related to the image you found. Bing Images includes all that and more. This page takes up the whole screen and sometimes includes features including the "Looks Like" section, where the search engine attempts to identify the subject of the image.

Other Web Sources

It's always helpful to search in a variety of places—you might find something you wouldn't have otherwise found. Beyond Google Image Search, there are many more image resources to explore on the open Web. For stock photos and other kinds of illustrative photos, **Flickr** can be a helpful source. Flickr also lets searchers filter results by Creative Commons license. Billions of images are hosted on Flickr, including those from many major organizations and governments. Many **museums** have extensive online image collections, though they are limited to the scope of their collections. The Metropolitan Museum of Art's collections in particular are high-quality and easy to search. The **Wikimedia Commons** is Wikipedia's online image repository. Like other projects from the Wikimedia Foundation, the images are generally free to use for a variety of purposes.

How to Search

When students begin searching for resources, librarians often assist them in brainstorming keywords. Image searches also benefit from this kind of assistance. When a student conducts any sort of search, it's helpful to remind them that they need to reverse-engineer their search results. Students should think about what sorts of words and phrases would appear in a helpful set of search results rather than thinking about what words or phrases *they'd* use to describe their research question. For example, a student is interested in researching the phenomenon of participation trophies. They're interested in finding out whether rewarding effort rather than success is beneficial or harmful to children. Rather than searching for words like "participation trophy," they'd think about what words a helpful result might use. Scholarly journals rarely use phrases like "participation trophy," so even though that's the phrase that came to the student's mind, it's *not* what they should use as a keyword. "Motivation" and "rewarding effort" would yield many more results that they might find helpful for their paper.

Doing this type of brainstorming, however, is different when thinking of images than it is with just text. Text documents like journal articles, books, and websites have different kinds of metadata from images. In addition, we use images differently from text, especially in research. Images usually have a much less distinct purpose than text does. It's not always a fact or phrase being cited within the body of an argument—they're used in a wide variety of ways, as discussed earlier in the "Crafting a Narrative" section.

There are two ways one can brainstorm keywords for image searches. The first way is to think of words that might appear in typical metadata fields. This is especially helpful for finding known images. If you have a specific person, place, or thing in mind, it's a safe bet that those words might appear in the title or description of the picture. The second way to brainstorm keywords is to think of words that might appear in an image's description. It's usually harder to search an image's contents, because unlike with the many full-text search tools that are available today, you can't usually search the contents of image—though there are some exceptions. Therefore, the searcher will need to think about what a helpful image might literally depict, instead of what they're trying to communicate with the image. If you were searching for an image of love, lots of images could be helpful—a picture of a couple embracing, or parents with their child, even a puppy looking up at the viewer. Those pictures could all be called many different things, none of which might use the word "love"—so you'd need to think about how others would describe the image rather than how you'd describe it.

ORGANIZING IMAGES

Keeping track of images (and their accompanying metadata) in an easy-to-use format is important! It's very tempting just to download anything you like or are considering using, but this can create problems later—especially when it comes time to properly cite or attribute those pictures. Saving images to your desktop or cloud storage might certainly work for projects that only require one or two images, but what if you're using a dozen? Do you try to rename all the image files, or maybe you just keep a running list of image information in a document? Both of those solutions can be a little clunky when dealing with larger amounts of images. Luckily, there are a few digital tools that will allow you to easily curate a collection of digital images and their metadata.

Sometimes, databases will have specific tools for organizing images. ARTstor, for example, has a system of Collections and Groups that will allow you to maintain a curated group of ARTstor images. Personal Collections also allow you to upload your own images outside of ARTstor's collection.

If you don't have access to ARTstor, don't worry; there are some great and free image resource curation apps out there that will allow you to help your students organize their resources. One of the most well-known of these is **Pinterest**, a popular social media site. Users can save image-based resources to various "boards," which is referred to as "pinning." Though students can search through Pinterest's search platform for images, I'd recommend they use other internet resources for scholarly research, as many of the images on Pinterest are unattributed. Most browsers will let students add the Pinterest

Save Button to their plugins. When students browse image-rich websites, they can use the Save button in their browser and add them to their boards. Clicking the Save button will display all of the images present on the page. The student can select the appropriate image, edit the caption as necessary, and add it to an existing or new board. By using the image's source website rather than repinning from another user on Pinterest, students can easily find their image sources again, as they can click on the image in their board to go back to the website.

Wakelet is another free image curation service. Wakelet is similar in concept to Pinterest; users can save images and media to different, user-created moodboards, which Wakelet calls collections. Wakelet is perhaps more ideal for use in a classroom setting, as its search functionality isn't as prominent or robust as it is on Pinterest. This means there's no distracting temptation for students to simply browse the posted images. Users can add websites, images, videos, and other forms of media to their collections by editing them and clicking on the green plus sign. Wakelet collections are easy to share via link by changing the visibility settings, can be customized, and are also usable for group projects, since you can invite contributors to work on your collections with you.

The most effective way to get students to understand the importance of organizing their image resources is by having them practice doing so. One great way to get students thinking about the importance of organizing and saving visual information is by hosting a digital curation workshop. See Chapter 6 for how to get started with using Wakelet for this fun library session. After utilizing the tools and methods discussed in this chapter and in the Digital Curation workshop, students will feel more comfortable with organizing their resources in future research projects. By organizing their image research, students can also easily archive their research for future use—this is particularly ideal for students who work on any kind of culminating projects, such as a thesis or portfolio of their work.

NOTES

1. ARTstor. "About ARTstor." http://www.artstor.org/about.
2. ARTstor. "Mission and History." https://www.artstor.org/about/mission-history.
3. Slobuski, Teresa. "Digital Image Databases: A Study from the Undergraduate Point of View." *Art Documentation: Journal of the Art Libraries Society of North America* 30, no. 2 (2011): 49–55.

3

Evaluating and Interpreting Images

The visually literate student should be able to evaluate and interpret the images they encounter on the internet. Not every image is suitable for academic use, just as not every website is appropriate for use as a source in research. First, we'll discuss how to evaluate images by examining their original source and accompanying metadata. Digital images are easy to share and are therefore often separated from their original metadata, so students can use Reverse Google Image Search to track an image back to its source. Once students have found some information about their image, they need to make a judgement call on whether or not they should use it. This book discusses how to use an adapted checklist approach, known as the ORCAS test, in order to make that judgement call.

Then, we'll cover how to interpret images. Image interpretation requires some special vocabulary that allows us to examine the building blocks of an image and gives us the right tools to write about those images. Images are created by people and can reflect the inherent biases and agendas of their creators. Being able to examine an image as a created object will allow students to spot these biases.

EVALUATING IMAGES

As librarians, we often speak about the importance of evaluating information we find before we share or use it. This is especially true of the information we find on the internet. Images, as a form of visual information, need to be evaluated just as much as textual information. In our digital world, it's incredibly easy to not only make images but edit them using powerful, widely available tools like Photoshop and share them with millions of people on the internet. Visual misinformation can spread like wildfire if viewers don't take a moment to make sure the content they're using is authoritative and reliable.

For example, during Hurricane Irene, a picture depicting a shark swimming down a freeway went viral. It's a shocking picture, seeing the dark, ominous shape of the shark where it normally doesn't belong. However, this picture is a hoax—it's composed of two images edited skillfully together to create one new, entirely fabricated image. The picture has since resurfaced after similar events, including 2012's Hurricane Sandy and 2017's Hurricane Harvey, each time being shared thousands of times. An edited image is an obvious type of visual misinformation, however. There are other, more insidious kinds of fake news images. People can, and sometimes do, use real images to represent situations that they don't picture. Teaching students to evaluate an image *and* its metadata will help them judge visual information much more effectively.

This section will discuss how to evaluate images. First, we'll cover how to find image information to evaluate. When evaluating an image for reliability, the searcher will need to look at not just the image but also its accompanying metadata. This is not always an easy thing to do, as images, in our digital world, are more often than not separated from their original source. We'll then discuss how to use Reverse Google Image Search to find an image's original source, which is an effective way to find missing metadata for an image. Once the searcher has some information to evaluate, the next step is to assess that information in order to make a judgement call on whether or not it's acceptable for academic use. This book takes a commonly used checklist approach in information evaluation—known as the CRAAP test—and adapts it for use with visual information.

Metadata

When evaluating images, students should first look for any accompanying metadata. Metadata is simply data about data, or in other words, information about a resource. Metadata will give students some context to the image that they're evaluating, so that they can better understand who created this image and what they can use it for. Ask students to see if there's a caption, or a credit, or an accompanying document that might provide additional information about their image. Look around the webpage. What can they find? Here's a list of metadata that commonly accompanies pictures:

- **Creator** refers to whoever created the image. However, "creator" can sometimes be tricky, especially with photographs. The credited "creator" is usually tied to the image's purpose. Is this an image of an object, or is the photo *itself* an image? If someone took a photo to document an object, the creator or the object will usually be credited. If the photo is an object in and of itself, whoever took that photo will usually be credited.

- **Title** refers to what the image is normally called. Not every image will have a title. Sometimes, a description, either by itself or in [brackets], will be used as a title. Other times, images are simply left untitled.
- **Date** refers to one of two things: when the image was created or when the object photographed was created.
- **Medium**, which might sometimes also be called material, refers to what the image was created with. It could list a traditional art medium, list oil on canvas or marble, or it could simply specify that it's a photo. Some photocentric websites, like Flickr, will list what type of camera (if known) created the image.
- **Description** is a few sentences or a brief phrase describing what the image pictures.
- **Size** refers to the dimensions of the image. It's most commonly used with pictures of digitized artwork, rather than born-digital images.

Image databases and image websites will often provide plenty of metadata about their collections. Oftentimes, they'll include additional information, such as repository, or where the image (or its pictured object) resides. Image search engines, including Google Image Search, will not always provide metadata about their search results. If a student cannot find any metadata, then they must go look for it. This usually means finding either the image's original source or an alternative descriptive source.

Students must become skeptics. Encourage your students to think deeply and critically about the images that they find in order to help them determine what their next steps should be. Is it time to start evaluating this image, or should I search for additional information about it? When they find an image, have them ask these kinds of questions in order to help them figure out if they need to search more deeply:

- Who do you think took this photo?
- Did this person repost this image?
- Is there any other information about this photo that you can find?
- Do you see a caption anywhere?

Finding Image Metadata: Looking for Image Sources

Once a student has determined that they must dig deeply into their image, it's time to see if they can find a different source for their images. Students will need to find either the image's original source or, failing that, an alternative descriptive source.

Original Sources

Images are very often separated from their original source due to the prevalence of reposting and sharing content, with or without credit. It's important to stress to your students that an image's original source is *not* where they originally found an image. The original source is where the image was first uploaded to the internet. For example, a student may find an image of a politician on Twitter. Upon further investigation, Twitter may have been where the student originally *found* the image, but it's not the image source.

Images are often reposted on social media sites, especially image-driven sites like Pinterest and Instagram. People also find and reuse images on all kinds of websites, from personal blogs to professional companies. Even if a website looks reputable, the creators may not be using original images. Image search engines in particular, including Google Image Search, find images across a variety of sources, which may or may not be using original images. This isn't a bad thing; it's perfectly acceptable to use and share information, including visual information. It's only that reposted images may not include a creator, date, or other useful metadata that you can use to assess an image's reliability.

Alternative Descriptive Sources

Even if a student can't find the original source, they still might be able to find a more descriptive source for their image. It's important to tell your students to not be discouraged when they can't track an image's original source. A digital image isn't an individual piece of art, whose provenance you can trace with determined research. An image may have been uploaded, shared multiple times, and then deleted from the original website. In addition, an image isn't always clearly published, like an article or book is.

A good alternative descriptive source is a reliable, authoritative website that has used the image in question and has provided some form of metadata. Have students look for other websites that have also used the image. Have students ask the same questions they did with their first image source in order to help them determine if there's enough metadata. In addition, they'll need to examine the new source itself. Is it more trustworthy than the source in which they first found the image? Make sure they investigate the new website thoroughly, looking for a publisher and investigating the authority of any creators. Search *beyond* the website too, and try to see if students can confirm information on another outlet. Some common examples of great alternative descriptive sources include but are not limited to image databases and news websites.

Using Reverse Google Image Search

Once a student has determined they need to find the image's original source, it's time to do some additional searching. Reverse Google Image Search is a powerful tool that you can use to track down a different, more useful image source.

First, students need to save a copy of the image they're investigating. On a Windows computer, you can right-click on an image, and then select Save Image As on the menu that appears. On a Mac computer, students can either right-click or control-click to get that same menu to appear. If any of your students are using mobile devices, they can simply tap and hold the image they wish to save; this should allow a menu to appear, where you can choose to save or download an image. Some websites and social media outlets do not allow you to save images; if this is the case, you can take a screenshot to save a copy of an image. Command + Shift + 4 on Mac will let you "snip" a portion of your screen, turning it into an image. Most Windows computers have some sort of snipping tool as well. On mobile phones, screenshotting procedures vary depending on the manufacturer.

Next, students will need to navigate to Google Image Search. Navigate to images.google.com, and instead of inputting keywords into the search bar, select the camera icon on the right side of the search bar. This uploads the image and allows Google to search for visually similar images. The option to upload images into Google Image Search does *not* appear on mobile devices, so students using phones and tablets will need to select "desktop site" in their browser.

Then, students will need to analyze the list of results that Google has found. The results list includes three basic sections: **possible related search, visually similar images**, and **pages that include matching images**. All three of these results can be useful in different kinds of ways, depending on what you're searching for:

- **Possible related searches** will usually appear at the top of the page of search results. To continue with more of these kinds of results, students will need to click the linked suggested search terms.
- **Visually similar images** will usually appear next on the page. This is a photo grid of images that look like, but are not, the image in question. Visually similar results may not always be helpful in finding a more descriptive source for an image, but they can be a useful tool in determining an image's originality. Students can see the full list of these results by clicking on the link above the photo grid.
- **Pages that include matching images** appear after visually similar images.

The best way to teach students to become image skeptics is by having them practice with real-world examples. The **Social Media Scavenger Hunt in Chapter 6** is a great way to engage students in image evaluation in any kind of class setting.

Evaluation Criteria

So, your students have an image and did enough sleuthing to come up with some metadata about their image. Now, it's time to analyze both the image and its data in order to make a judgement call on whether or not it's suitable for academic use.

Over the years, librarians have developed a number of different methods of evaluating information. The CRAAP test is a common example. CRAAP is an acronym consisting of different words used to evaluate a resource's suitability for use in academic research. CRAAP stands for Currency, Relevance, Authority, Accuracy, and Purpose. The CRAAP test is usually used as a checklist of criteria to consider when judging information.[1]

While CRAAP was designed to be used for text documents, it can be modified to work for images. When it's time for students to evaluate visual media, ask them to apply the ORCAS test. After finding an image that they intend to use in their academic work, evaluate the image by the following set of criteria:

- **Originality** asks the searcher to determine whether or not the image has been edited. Are there portions of the picture that distinctly stand out? Is this a composite of multiple images?
- **Relevance** asks the searcher to consider how the image relates to their research need.
- **Currency** refers to when the image was created or the photograph was taken. People do have a tendency to reuse and share old photos, which can become problematic.
- **Authority** refers to who created this image. Can you verify that the photo was taken by a reliable source? Authority can be more difficult to assess in an image, particularly in photos. It's perhaps more important to look at the publisher of the image, rather than the photographer.
- **Subject matter** refers to what the picture seemingly shows. Is a person, place, or object pictured? If so, can you confirm its identity? A good description in the image's metadata can help the student clearly define an image's subject matter.

Like with the CRAAP test, every factor in the ORCAS test must be considered. Even if one or two of the factors pass the test, the image as a whole still may be unsuitable. For example, say a student is researching the economic effects of the catastrophic 2010 flood in Nashville. A student may find a photo of flood damage from *The New York Times*. At first, such a photo might seem authoritative and relevant. However, on closer inspection, it might actually be a photo of the 2017 Houston flood, perhaps in an article about several deadly floods in the United States. Without reading the photo's caption to confirm its subject matter, the student might not realize that this image doesn't pass the ORCAS test.

If you want to host an image evaluation one-off session, you could have students evaluate the image of their choice. A sample ORCAS worksheet, along with instructions, can be found in Chapter 6.

INTERPRETING IMAGES

Evaluating image metadata isn't a foreign concept to us librarians. As discussed earlier, it's fairly similar to the kind of information evaluation we teach in information literacy sessions. The act of interpreting an image's content might not be as intuitive, but it's an essential component of image evaluation.

Sometimes, people have a tendency to accept images, especially photographs, as visual representations of the truth. We use phrases like "pics or it didn't happen," "photographic evidence," and "seeing is believing" to express our trust in images. However, images, just like text, are objects that are created by humans. This means that images can be biased and manipulative. Image choice can affect how we, the viewers, feel about something.

When students evaluate text documents, they need to evaluate both the metadata about the document and the document itself. Students need to do the same with images. We've discussed how to evaluate image metadata, so now we'll cover how to interpret the image itself.

Image Vocabulary

When you interpret textual information, you look at how the author uses language to make the reader feel a certain way about the information being conveyed. When you interpret images, you need to look at how the creator has used aesthetic vocabulary to make the viewer feel a certain way about the subject. Aesthetic vocabulary refers to the basic components that make up every piece of visual information. Though aesthetic vocabulary may seem irrelevant to those outside of the fine arts disciplines, it's actually a vital part in image interpretation. Understanding *how* someone has created an image and why certain aspects of the image are highlighted will let you better understand why it makes you feel a certain way.

One thing to note: students should take care to use aesthetic vocabulary to interpret the image as a whole, rather than just focusing on one or two aspects of the image that stand out. The interplay of line, space, and color within an image creates a narrative, and students run the risk of simplifying the image too much if they don't consider all parts of it.

Line

A line is, essentially, just "a relatively narrow, elongated mark."[2] Line is one of the simplest and most basic building blocks in all images, and it's also one of the tools a creator can use to emphasize certain parts of an image, as lines draw the viewer's eyes along their length, directing attention to their ends. Lines that converge around a certain part of the image look focused and sharp. A *person* situated in that convergence might look in command and competent, for example. The converse is also true: if the lines in the image are seemingly randomly placed, the image might feel chaotic.

Lines are everywhere in images and can take a variety of different forms. Lines can be actual drawn lines, or they can be linear objects within the image. Pointing fingers, the horizon, extended arms, roads, signs, and more are all different ways that lines can appear. Lines can also be implied, like line of sight. There might not be an actual drawn mark from someone's gaze, but our eyes follow it just as they would with a real line.

Photo 3.1 is a good example of how a photographer can use line to make an image look chaotic. There's a variety of visible lines, including the gazes of the seven visible people, a pointed finger on an outstretched arm, and a phone cord. All of the lines are unfocused in this image; they don't converge in one single area.

This photo depicts former U.S. President George Bush receiving the initial news about the September 11th terrorist attack on the World Trade Center. The chaotic nature of this image tells a story and was almost certainly a conscious decision by the photographer. It's a stressful, anxious moment, and the picture reflects that. It reflects the chaotic shock that most viewers felt when they, too, heard the news about the September 11th attacks. If the president and his companions had looked professional and focused, they might not have been as relatively vulnerable as they are in this image.

PHOTO 3.1. 9/11: President George W. Bush Receives Information Regarding Terrorist Attacks. September 11, 2001.
Source: National Archives and Records Administration.

Of course, an image creator can also use line to make a person look focused and commanding. Let's take a look at Photo 3.2. Though this image was taken on the same day as Photo 3.1, it has a very different mood to it, which can be attributed, in part, to the different treatment of line. The lines in this photo (including the crowd's gaze, outstretched arms, cameras, and microphones) are centered in the president at the podium.

This moment tells a different story. It looks organized and focused, just like how the Bush administration wanted their response to the terrorist attacks to be. Had the photographer waited a few moments or snapped a picture as Bush finished speaking, it might not have the tight, commanding focus that this image does.

Space

Space is another important concept in aesthetic vocabulary. It's more than just the empty areas of an image; space is a way to describe the different layers of meaning within an image. There are two kinds of space: **positive space** and **negative space**. Positive space refers to the subject of the image, whereas negative space refers to the background.

PHOTO 3.2. 9/11: President George W. Bush Delivers Remarks on Terrorist Attacks from Barksdale Air Force Base. September 11, 2001.
Source: National Archives and Records Administration.

Positive and negative space can be very clear in some pictures. In a basic portrait of an individual, the person will represent the positive space, and everything else will be the background. In other pictures, it might not be so clear. Space is all about interpretation, so some students may have differing ideas from one another about where the positive space begins and where the negative space begins. When trying to determine what, exactly, is the positive space in an image, ask your students questions like:

- What is the main focus of this picture?
- What do you think the photographer was trying to take a picture of?
- What do you think the background is in this picture?

By manipulating the positive and negative space, an image creator can make a viewer see the subject from their perspective. If the positive space takes up most of the room in the image, it can look large and important. If the negative space takes up more room, the positive space can look small and overwhelmed.

In Photo 3.3, the photographer has used both positive and negative space to emphasize the size and majesty of the trees. The people at the bottom can be

PHOTO 3.3. [Deodars at Annandale, Simla]. 1858–61, Unknown.
Source: Gilman Collection, Purchase, Gynthia Hazen Polsky Gift, 2005. Courtesy of the
Metropolitan Museum of Art.

considered the positive space, while the trees can be considered the negative
space. The small size of the people makes them look especially small when
compared to the soaring height of the trees.

If you flip your interpretations of the positive and negative space in this
image, it reads much the same. The trees being considered the positive space
makes them look especially large because they make up the majority of the
image. It's not *how* you define the different kinds of space: it's how the different kinds of space interact with one another.

Color

There are two different terms we mean when we refer to color: **hue** and
value. Value refers to how light or dark the color is, while hue refers to the
actual shade of the color. Dark, burgundy red, ruby red, and pastel pink are
all different values of the same color: red. Blue, yellow, and brown, on the
other hand, are all different examples of hues. When students interpret an
image's use of color, they need to be able to use words like hue and value to

describe *how* the artist is manipulating color in highlighting certain parts of the visual narrative.

Color can draw our attention in two ways. Different hues can highlight different parts of an image; they can stand out and command our attention. A lone figure dressed in red in a crowd of dark-suited individuals stands out because it differs sharply from everything else. Different values can be used to imply different kinds of lighting, which can lend the image a certain kind of mood. A darker photo with low lighting might look more foreboding than an airy, light-filled room, for example.

Photo 3.4 showcases how a photographer can use color to highlight the subject of an image. There are many things going on in this historic snapshot; there's a lot of busy-looking vegetation, there's a flowing river next to a rocky outcrop, and there's a white heron. Your eyes are immediately drawn to the bird, as its white feathers are very distinct against the dark water behind it. That sharp contrast catches our eyes, unlike the busier shades of gray that represent the plant life.

PHOTO 3.4. The Heron. 1853–56, John Dillwyn Llewelyn.
Source: Gilman Collection, Gift of The Howard Gilman Foundation, 2005. Courtesy of the Metropolitan Museum of Art.

While *The Heron* represents a fairly innocuous use of color, color can be used to make the viewer feel sympathetic or distant. A figure shrouded in darkness can look foreboding or moody, while a person swathed in light may look brighter and more accessible. Highlighting a bird in nature is one thing; making a political candidate look friendlier or forbidding is another.

Other Terms

Line, space, and color are three basic concepts that appear in all images and are a useful starting point for college students who are learning how to become visually literate researchers. There are, however, a number of other aesthetic vocabulary terms that you can use to analyze images. If a group of students are ready to delve deeper into image interpretation, you may want to introduce some of the following terms:

- **Repetition.** Are figures, lines, shapes, and other elements repeated throughout the picture? A repeated element is emphasized, which naturally draws the viewer's attention.
- **Balance.** Sometimes images will have clear symmetry, which lends a sense of balance. Balanced images are calmer and more harmonious than unbalanced ones—which can subtly discomfort the reader.
- **Scale.** Scale is often tied to space. How is the creator using our sense of scale to change our perspective of the image's space?

Activity

As always, the best way to get your students thinking about how to interpret and write about images is to have them actually participate. In Chapter 6, you'll find the News Image Analysis Discussion posts, an online discussion board activity that you can use to start a conversation about image choices in the news, as well as get students accustomed to interpreting images with a critical eye.

Image Context

So . . . you and your students have analyzed the artistic details in an image. Now, it's time to look at the bigger picture, so to speak, and examine the context that informed the image's creation, as well as its current use.

What Is Context?

Context refers to the circumstances surrounding an image. What were the social, historical, political, and other circumstances that inform how and why this image was created? Images, as discussed earlier, are a product of the people who have created them. People, in turn, are shaped by a number

PHOTO 3.5. David Johnston at Coldwater II, May 17, 1980.
Source: U.S. Geological Survey.

of societal and institutional factors. We discussed how a creator can use the building blocks of images—line, space, and color—to create a visual document that tells a certain kind of story. In researching the context surrounding an image, we can better understand why a creator may have made an image a certain way and how that knowledge changes our perception of the image's subject matter.

Take, for example, the image you see in Photo 3.5. Try to interpret the subject of the image based on just what you see in the picture. It's a man, seated casually near a vehicle. He looks relaxed, and the sun seems to be brightly shining. Several large trees loom in the background, or negative space. It seems to be just an ordinary portrait of a man, perhaps camping or otherwise enjoying a day spent in nature.

However, if we interpret the photo based on what we can learn from its metadata, a much different kind of picture emerges. There's a date and title—David Johnston at Coldwater II. This gives us some information on the **historic context** of this image and allows us to place the photo in the time in which it was made. This is more than just a photo of a man camping in nature. Further research on the date—May 17, 1980—and the place—Coldwater II—lets us place the photo in the time and space in which it was created. In this case, Coldwater II was an observation post by Mount St. Helens for the U.S. Geological Survey, and May 17, 1980, was the day before Mount St. Helens erupted. We can also research the name in the title, David Johnston. In this case, we learn that David Johnston was a volcanologist who tragically passed in the volcano's eruption.[3] While it wouldn't be an appropriate image for use in a text discussing the beauty of nature, it would perfectly illustrate the concept of sudden change and the destructive power of nature. Without understanding the context for this image, we could have badly misused it.

Interpreting Context

In interpreting context, students will need to use the metadata that they located earlier. Metadata can offer important clues that allow the viewer to situate an image within the time and place it was created. When they're ready to start the interpretation, ask your students some questions to spark a discussion on the image's context:

- Look at the date. What do we know about this time period?
- Who's the creator?
- Why would they have taken this picture?
- What can we find out about them?
- What is the title of this picture?
- Does it offer us any more clues?
- How does any of this change your reading of the subject matter within the image?

Altogether, this discussion can help your students interpret the true subject of an image and make a thoughtful, informed decision on *how* to use the image effectively and truthfully.

Activity

Juxtapose JS is a free, easy-to-use digital humanities tool that allows you to compare two images. You can go to the Juxtaposition Group Activity in Chapter 6 for an idea about how to use this tool to teach the importance of understanding context in image evaluation.

NOTES

1. Lenker, Mark. "Developmentalism: Learning as the Basis for Evaluating Information." *Portal* 17, no. 4 (2017): 721–37. doi:10.1353/pla.2017 .0043.
2. Sayre, Henry M. *Writing about Art*. Upper Saddle River: Pearson Prentice Hall, 2009.
3. "The Legacy of David A. Johnston." https://www.usgs.gov/observatories /cascades-volcano-observatory/legacy-david-a-johnston.

4

Designing and Communicating with Images

The visually literate student should be able to edit and create images. Making images in our digital world is a far less intimidating task than it used to be. Students can utilize a variety of hardware to create beautiful, useful images for any kind of project, with no traditional artistic skill required. In many cases, students even already have access to powerful hardware in the form of smartphone cameras. But students should be able to edit images in addition to simply taking pictures. Editing images is a valuable tool that will allow your students to tell their narratives more effectively. Software is usually needed to edit images, and there's a huge variety of software available. This chapter will make that choice a little less daunting by providing criteria you should consider, as well as recommending some current choices. We'll then discuss how to approach image self-evaluation with your students.

We'll also cover how to integrate more visual literacy instruction into your information literacy curriculums. Many students are already working with and needing help with images, so locating these students is key. Visual literacy is suited for a wide variety of library instruction, from the one-shot session to in-depth, semester-long faculty collaboration. Finding these faculty members who already work with images across the disciplines and being able to offer them a flexible menu of instruction is the key to getting the word out about visual literacy on your campus.

MAKING IMAGES

The ability to effectively edit and create images will allow your students to become effective and ethical visual storytellers. Though sometimes pictures are seen as primarily decorative, this is clearly not the case. Images are also an important part of learning and of crafting a research-based narrative.

For one thing, images make things more compelling. Specifically, images make text more compelling. Time and time again, studies have shown images increase comprehension and understanding of the topic they accompany.[1] Images are also more memorable than other forms of information, making them useful for any student. Pictures imprint themselves more effectively in the brain, since we can recall both an image and whatever words were associated with it, rather than just text.[2] A student may be more successful in learning about a topic if they're presented with visual information in addition to text, making images an important part of the research process. The goal of research, after all, is to learn something!

Seeing pictures can clearly make textual content more engaging, but that's not all they can do. The act of creating images can also allow students to understand some of the other facets of visual literacy more clearly. For example, actually using image vocabulary—like line, space, and color—can show how effective these tools can be in crafting a visual narrative.

But not only is the act of viewing images compelling, the act of creating images is compelling. It allows students to be thoughtful and creative and use a different kind of skill set. Just like how everyone needs to write, everyone needs to be able to effectively engage in our highly visual world. Everyone needs to be able to create images in one form or another. Students and professionals in a variety of disciplines are now expected to be able to create attractive presentations, for example. Therefore, the visually literate student should be able to make images—and the library can help with this.

Making images today requires only two basic components: the necessary hardware to actually create an image and then software to fine-tune that picture and craft it into something that can add to your narrative.

Hardware

In the past, students lacking the materials and training to draw and draft images were reliant upon someone's else's skill, and often, interpretation. Luckily, this isn't the case in the digital era, where the ability to create effective images today requires little more than a computer and some software. Today, we use a variety of tools to create digital images.

Providing the right tools for creating images can help establish your library as a center for image creation. This could, in turn, help spark conversations and collaboration between the library and other faculty members, once they know that they can send students to your library for assistance.

There are a number of image creation tools available today:

- **Cameras** allow students to take high-quality photos. Cameras, of course, come in many different forms, from basic point-and-shoot cameras for the common user, to complex and expensive or digital single lens reflex cameras (DSLR). DSLR cameras, used by professionals, allow users to take high-quality, high-resolution images.
- **Tablets or iPads** allow students to draw illustrations or annotate existing ones. Tablets have cameras and touchscreens that can be used for image creation. Sometimes, additional stylus accessories can be acquired to help users utilize the touchscreen for image creation more effectively.
- **Digital writing tablets or graphics drawing tablets** are similar to iPad-style tablets, but they're not quite the same. This kind of tablet comes with a stylus, and people use it by drawing on the screen, and they typically watch a computer monitor to see their work. It's not a computing device in and of itself, but a peripheral accessory to be used with a computer (like a mouse). This is a specialized piece of equipment and is not commonly utilized by those outside of the art and design field.
- **Video cameras** allow students to take videos. Though this book is primarily concerned with pictures and photographs, video is an important part of today's digital visual landscape. Short videos can also be converted to animated looping GIFs, which is helpful in some web formats and presentations.

If you have a limited budget, you may choose not to invest in hardware at all. Hardware, besides being an expensive up-front investment, requires maintenance, a technology check-out policy and planning, and, of course, regular upgrades. Many students, if not the vast majority, carry around a smartphone every day. Over 3.5 billion people own smartphones, and the United States is one of the countries with the highest number of smartphone users.[3] Smartphones usually have powerful cameras (and can take videos), are far more familiar to students, and are therefore more accessible. Instead, consider finding some software that your students can use for image editing.

Software

If you want to invest in image creation and editing materials for your library, software might be a great use of your resources and time. While many people already have access to the basic hardware they need to create images, not everyone has access to programs that can modify those images.

You might be asking yourself: If my students have the capability to take photos, do they *really* need image editing software? Isn't "photoshopping" for making fake, deceptive images? While Photoshop and other image editing software can be used to make manipulative images, it can also be a helpful tool that allows students to tell their research narratives more effectively.

Take, for example, Photo 4.1. This image is an aerial view of the Belmont University campus, which was then known as the Ward-Belmont College. In this image, we not only see the campus but also the surrounding area, including nearby streets, houses, and other buildings. If you were making a presentation on how Belmont's campus has changed over the years or about the importance of the Ward-Belmont College in Nashville, this might be a really great image to use. However, it's not perfect. If you're unfamiliar with Belmont's campus or this particular neighborhood in Nashville, it's difficult to determine where the campus actually is. If we crop this image, we can make the subject more focused and easier for the viewer to determine what, exactly, they're looking at. In all likelihood, the presenter would need to spend some time explaining where the campus begins and ends in this photo.

PHOTO 4.1. Aerial View. 1950. Belmont University Special Collections.
Source: Image used with permission from Belmont University.

PHOTO 4.2. Aerial View. Cropped. 1950. Belmont University Special Collections.
Source: Image used with permission from Belmont University.

Now, take a look at Photo 4.2. Photo 4.2 is the same photo as Photo 4.1, only it's been cropped. The picture now just shows Ward-Belmont's 1950 campus, with the extraneous neighborhood houses trimmed out. There's no need to explain what is campus and what isn't. It's more focused, with the subject front and center, taking up the majority of the foreground. It's a simple change, but an effective one.

Cropping is just one example of why a student might need image editing software. Students may want to annotate images with text or shapes, modify the color, or remove background scenes. Using these kinds of tools lets students work with the basics of image vocabulary themselves and can give firsthand experience as to how powerful line, color, space, and more can be. These kinds of edits can also make an image's intended message clearer to their prospective audience, so students should have access to software, when possible.

A huge variety of image creation software is available, which can make choosing the right kind of software seem like quite a task. Figuring out what you need the software for, who's using it, and what kind of resources you have to purchase (and support) the software will help you narrow down your search. Ask yourself these kinds of questions when selecting an appropriate image editor:

- Who's going to be the primary user of this software? Think about your student population. Do you have a diverse student population, with mixed levels of ability, or do you have a group of advanced design students, who need high-powered software? Considering the possible expertise of your students will help you decide what kinds of capabilities it should have.

- What's my budget? Software can be quite an expense, with some even requiring a yearly subscription commanding the same budgetary resources as a database subscription would. Other software is available for a lower price, or even free. Knowing what your library is willing and able to pay for is a key factor in selecting software.

- What are my limitations? Try to think of any obstacles you may encounter. For example, will you be allowed to install new software on your library's computers, or will you have to go through a lengthy approval process? If so, you could consider linking to a number of web-based image editors, rather than installing an actual program on your computer. Limitations vary for every library, so think widely about the kinds of issues you could encounter.

- How can I help people with this software? Is training available or other resources I can provide for those who need guidance? You don't need to be an expert yourself, but you still may need to troubleshoot some basic issues with any piece of software used in your library. If the software you acquire is professional-grade, this may be a more difficult task.

Now that you know what you're looking for in image software, let's look at some of the popular choices that are available. This list, while not exhaustive, will give you an overview of the landscape of image software. These popular choices have been divided into two categories: those that you can at least begin to use for free and those you must pay to access at all.

Free Software

Image creation doesn't have to be expensive; indeed, there's a number of free image editing software that students can use.

- **Canva. Free to use** (but with subscriptions available). **Web-based.** Canva is a basic image editor that allows anyone to create sleek images through the use of its stock images and designer templates. Canva can perform some basic tasks like cropping, but does not have many high-powered features. Its primary value lies in its templates, which can be used to easily and quickly produce an attractively designed presentation or poster.

- **darktable** is an entirely **free-to-use** photo editor. It's designed for working with original photographs. With darktable, users can organize, sort, and edit their photos. It can perform most of the tasks that users would require, including offering many options for tweaking the color and contrast of your photos. It's **installable on Mac, PC, and Linux.** It's a good alternative to Adobe's Lightroom, if you don't have room in your budget for pricey software subscriptions.

- **GIMP,** or GNU Image Manipulation Program, is open source and entirely **free to use. It's installable on Mac, PC, and Linux machines.** GIMP is one of the most powerful free image editing software programs available today. If your students need to perform complex tasks but you don't have the budget for a paid piece of software, GIMP might be an ideal choice.

Purchasable Software

Depending on how interested your library is in working with visual resources, you might want to consider investing in image editing software.

- **Adobe Creative Suite** is the industry standard and one of the most well-known vendors of image software. Adobe has several pieces of software, each one with a specialized purpose. While there are many Adobe products, Photoshop and Lightroom are the most relevant to a librarian looking to help students access image software.
- **Photoshop** is perhaps the most famous of these. It's a powerful image editor that is capable of editing just about everything on any kind of image. Photoshop is fairly complicated to use, so users without experience in using it specifically may have trouble using this piece of software. If you're working with design students, they may require this kind of advanced software. Other student populations, however, may be best served by other options.
- **Lightroom** is a similar piece of software, but it's focused on editing and organizing photographs specifically. In Lightroom, unlike Photoshop, a user can also import and catalog their photos, along with retouching them as desired. One of the benefits of Adobe products is that since Adobe is so well-known, there are plenty of options for support. There are lots of books and e-resources, such as Lynda.com, about learning how to use different Adobe products. Adobe products work on both Macs and PCs, but there's a catch: the price. One of the biggest drawbacks to using Adobe products is the fact that they require a **yearly subscription,** so your library would need to commit to paying for Adobe every year.
- **Photoshop Elements** is another piece of Adobe software, but it's one that deserves its own bullet. Photoshop Elements is a pared-down version of the professional-grade Adobe Photoshop. It can accomplish most of what you'd need to do to edit images, including removing

backgrounds and touching up color. It's simpler and easier to use than Adobe Photoshop.[4] Unlike Adobe Creative Suite, Photoshop Elements is available for a **one-time fee** instead of a subscription model.

- **Affinity Photo** is another piece of image editing software. It can do most of what Photoshop can accomplish, including adjusting color and adding layers to images, but doesn't have some of the advanced features that programs like Photoshop have for importing and exporting images or customizing the interface.[5] Affinity Photo is a downloadable piece of software for both Macs and PCs with a **one-time, fairly affordable price**—less than $100.

- **Paint Shop Pro** is yet another popular image editing software. Paint Shop Pro has lots of great image editing capabilities, including a sophisticated smart crop tool, and plenty of photo editing effects. While Corel has some products that work on Mac computers, Paint Shop Pro does not, as it's Windows only.[6] Paint Shop Pro also has a **one-time fee** of less than $100 instead of Adobe's subscription model.

EVALUATING YOUR OWN IMAGE USE

Students should be able to do more than simply create an image. They need to be able to see how the image adds to their narrative and what they might be able to do to improve it. In addition to creating images, effective visual communicators should be able to evaluate their own image use. We've already discussed how to evaluate *other* people's images for reliability, authority, and other indicators of quality, but students need to be critical of their own use of visual materials.

Image use self-evaluation should occur when a student has drafted their project or paper but has yet to turn it in. Image use self-evaluation is similar to, but not exactly the same as, general image evaluation. Self-evaluation should occur after the project has been completed, or at least drafted, but before they turn it in or deliver their presentation. Students should think about what the image they chose is doing for the project or paper. They can ask themselves questions like: What does this image choice add to my argument? Is it clear to other people? Is there something I can do to improve what this image is communicating?

How you should approach image self-evaluation should be determined by whether the image in question was found on the internet or was an original creation by the student. For found images, you should rely on both evaluation characteristics and the interpretation of the image, both of which are discussed at length in Chapter 3. Questions about authority and subject matter are particularly useful here. It's always useful to double-check that the

PHOTO 4.3. Cats and Affection Presentation Slide. 2020.
Source: Courtesy of the author.

image is from an authoritative source. Would your audience consider that source authoritative? Does that add to or take away from the argument? For original creations, students should primarily focus on the interpretation of the image, as well as the S in ORCAS—subject matter. Is the subject matter clear in this image? And how does the image portray this subject? These are two questions a self-evaluator should ask of their creation.

Let's look at an example. Take Photo 4.3, which is a slide from a sample presentation about how cats are misunderstood as aloof, due to the fact that they express affection differently from dogs. In this slide, the creator lists several ways a cat might express affection and has included an image of a cat. In this image, the cat is purring while seated. The photographer may know that the cat is relaxed and affectionate, but the image doesn't necessarily make this apparent. The **subject matter** isn't clear. The image was chosen with not necessarily the audience in mind.

In Photo 4.4, the slide has been amended. The image included has been changed to that of a cat lying on its back, with its belly exposed. The subject matter in this image is much clearer to the audience: an exposed cat belly, according to the slide, is a clear sign of affection.

If you're helping students evaluate their own image use, another great way to approach this kind of image evaluation is by utilizing a peer-review system. One of the best ways to understand how other people see something is

PHOTO 4.4. Cats and Affection Presentation Slide. 2020.
Source: Courtesy of the author.

to actually *ask* other people, after all. If you're an embedded librarian and are working with students who are engaged in image-based projects, Chapter 6's Image Design Studio Critique is a great way to have students think about how effective their image use and choices are. The Image Design Studio Critique is a paired activity that gets students thinking about how a peer has used an image in a project and can be a helpful activity for students needing extra assistance in this aspect of visual literacy.

VISUAL LITERACY INSTRUCTION IN HIGHER EDUCATION

You might be asking yourself *how* you can implement more visual literacy instruction. But the truth is, many students are already using images in their research and coursework—and need assistance in finding and using those images properly. Look for opportunities across the disciplines—do you know of a faculty member with an interest in digital humanities? When you provide research assistance to students, ask them about what kind of project they're working on—some kinds of projects, like a blog or other kind of website, or a presentation, might lead you towards faculty who'd be grateful and interested in some visual literacy instruction.

Once you start seeing students using images, it's time to connect with the faculty asking them to use images. There are two ways you can start embedding more visual literacy instruction at your institution: **short-term** and **long-term** instruction. Short-term instruction refers to the kind of instruction that usually lasts less than a day. While short-term instruction is useful and relevant, you should also seek out opportunities to work with students on a more long-term basis, usually in the form of a faculty collaboration.

Short-Term Instruction

Short-term instruction is the bread and butter of library instruction. Every instruction librarian, at some point or another, will conduct a one-shot instruction session, where they visit a class and take over the lesson for the day. Short-term instruction can take several forms, including the aforementioned one-shot library instruction visit. Events, workshops, and asynchronous videos are all additional forms of short-term instruction—they happen once, and then the instruction is concluded. The librarian will generally not visit the class or group of students again.

There are many benefits to using short-term instruction to teach about visual literacy. First and foremost, it's a familiar format to us librarians. One-shots and workshops are something that most librarians have conducted; if you're trying to teach a skill that's new to you (like image evaluation), then a familiar instruction format may allow you to better focus on the new subject content. Short-term instruction also allows you to meet with a larger number of students. Instead of working with the same 30 students all semester, you get the opportunity to have an impact on hundreds of students. If you want to start getting many students to think about visual literacy, implementing a series of one-shots may have a greater impact for your time. Short-term instruction is also usually an easier sell to your faculty, since they don't have to give up too much of their limited class time.

The biggest drawback to short-term instruction is that you only get a very limited amount of time with your students. This means that you can't always go in-depth into a topic, so it's necessary for short-term instruction to have a clear focus.

Many of the activities in Chapter 6 are ideally suited for short-term instruction, because they focus on one specific aspect of visual literacy. If you're looking to integrate some short-term visual literacy instruction into your curriculum, the best way to do so is to communicate with your faculty. This will allow you to figure out what the faculty member ultimately wants from instruction. If an instructor wants you to help their students evaluate images, you can figure what they really mean by that with a conversation. Do they want their students to find reliable, authoritative photos, or do they want to interpret the implicit bias in a set of news photos? This will let you know if you should focus on image evaluation (via ORCAS) or image interpretation, for example.

Long-Term Instruction

Long-term instruction is library instruction that takes place over a period of time, rather than just one day. A librarian who teaches a for-credit course, a three-day workshop for graduate students, and a semester-long faculty–librarian collaboration on a research assignment are all examples of long-term library instruction. Long-term library instruction has several key benefits. It's ideally suited for more complicated topics. Since you have more time to interact with students, you may feel more comfortable working with a complicated topic, such as visual literacy in general, rather than just one or two different aspects of visual literacy.

However, long-term instruction isn't always the best solution for trying to get more visual literacy instruction onto your campus. It requires many more resources, including time, space, and mental bandwidth. Long-term instruction requires much more dedicated time, both your time and the instructor's, if you're working with someone else.

If you'd like to begin utilizing some long-term visual literacy instruction, one of the most exciting and fruitful ways to do so is through a faculty–librarian collaboration. Faculty collaboration is a great way to embed some visual literacy instruction directly into a scaffolded research assignment. In this kind of collaboration, a librarian works with a faculty member to design an assignment and provide instruction at several key points in the semester. During these key points, the librarian will often lead a class, providing instruction and sometimes an assignment involving just a portion of the larger assignment. Research paper alternatives are a great example of this kind of collaboration.

Consulting with faculty on research assignments is a great way to embed visual literacy instruction into the college classroom. If you're interested in speaking with one of your faculty members about this kind of collaboration, check out the StoryMap Research Project in Chapter 6 for some inspiration on how to use this research paper alternative on your campus.

NOTES

1. Dewan, Pauline. "Words versus Pictures: Leveraging the Research on Visual Communication." *Partnership: The Canadian Journal of Library and Information Practice and Research* 10, no. 1 (2015): 2.
2. Paivio, Allan, Timothy B. Rogers, and Padric C. Smythe. "Why Are Pictures Easier to Recall Than Words?" *Psychonomic Science* 11, no. 4 (1968): 137–38.
3. Statista. "Smartphone Users Worldwide 2020." https://www.statista.com/statistics/330695/number-of-smartphone-users-worldwide.

4. Muchmore, Michael. "Adobe Photoshop Elements Review." PCMAG.
    https://www.pcmag.com/reviews/adobe-photoshop-elements?test_uuid
    =03VgQESfXzdGbpM9u5nO4tq&test_variant=a.
5. PCMAG. "Serif Affinity Photo Review." https://www.pcmag.com/reviews
    /serif-affinity-photo?test_uuid=03VgQESfXzdGbpM9u5nO4tq&test
    _variant=a.
6. Muchmore, Michael. "Corel PaintShop Pro Review." PCMAG. https://
    www.pcmag.com/reviews/corel-paintshop-pro?test_uuid=03VgQESfXz
    dGbpM9u5nO4tq&test_variant=a.

Citation and Ethics for Images

The visually literate student should be able to document images they use in whatever style is used in their discipline. Documenting resources and crediting their sources are very important parts of information literacy. This is just as important in visual literacy, too. Chapter 3 stressed the importance of metadata in image evaluation; this chapter discusses how students can use that metadata to properly credit an image's source. Documenting images allows students to ensure that anyone who views their research, including their professor, is able to properly evaluate their images. This chapter will also go over the difference between image citation and image attribution and when to utilize them. It'll also provide examples of image citation and attribution, so that you're prepared to help your students (and faculty!) with a variety of different image documentation needs.

It's not enough to just cite images. Students also need to be able to understand copyright issues that affect image use. Visually literate students should use images ethically by adhering to these copyright laws and guidelines. There are many circumstances in which students use images, from basic classroom use, to campus publications, to public presentations, to using them on a public website. This chapter will go over different kinds of guidelines that can help students (again, and faculty) determine whether or not an image *should* be used.

DOCUMENTING IMAGES

First, students need to be able to properly document the images that they use. Documentation and citation are among the more difficult topics to approach in library instruction. I usually dread the citation conversation with students, because it's always hard to teach something students so obviously don't enjoy. It is, however, an important and necessary lesson. Documentation allows students to provide proof of their research efforts, something that an instructor obviously needs and values. It also allows students to see the work that goes into creating a research document. One of the things that students tend to gravitate toward in evaluating websites and articles is the amount of research that has gone into its creation. Images are just as valuable of a form of information as text documents, so these resources need just as much attention in the documentation.

The first and most important part of documenting an image is making sure you have all the accompanying metadata for that image. The metadata, like the title, creator, and date, will provide the information needed to formulate the citation or attribution. This is not a difficult task if the image in question is from a well-organized and documented source, like an image database or a museum website. This will probably not be the case, however, on the many images found across the internet. If you and your students need some help finding the appropriate metadata for an image, be sure to check out Chapter 3: Evaluating and Interpreting Images, which includes some helpful tips on tracking down lost image metadata. Then, you'll need to figure out what a student is trying to do: **cite** an image or give an image an **attribution**.

Citation

Image citation refers to when students need to cite images in a specific style, such as APA, Chicago, or MLA. If a student is writing a paper in a specific style, their image citations should follow the same rules as their other cited materials. Citation is something many students find difficult to master. In student survey feedback, I consistently notice students saying they need more help with citation. Image citation is even more difficult to deal with than everyday, document-based citation. The rules regarding image citation are not usually as detailed as they need to be, especially for digital image citation.

In Photo 5.1, we have an example of an image with an accompanying image citation. In this image, the caption features a properly formatted citation in APA style. However, creating a citation for an image is not always as easy as it may seem, since the rules for image citation are often difficult to apply to digital images. Let's look at some of the common citation style guides and see how their guidelines apply to digital images.

APA Style

The seventh edition of the *Publication Manual of the American Psychological Association* outlines the basics of writing, publishing, and referencing in

PHOTO 5.1. Wolcott, M. P. (1939). [Haircutting in Front of General Store and Post Office on Marcella Plantation, Mileston, Mississippi] [Photograph]. The Metropolitan Museum of Art, New York, NY, United States. https://www.metmuseum.org/art/collection/search/265311.
Source: Courtesy of the Metropolitan Museum of Art.

APA style. Chapter 10, which is entitled "Reference Examples," is the most relevant for most students trying to figure out the intricacies of citation in APA.

The APA manual does a good job of attempting to demystify image citation and is probably the easiest to understand of the three major styles. In Chapter 10, there's a section entitled "Audiovisual Media," and within this section is a subsection entitled "Visual Works." Here, students will find a variety of helpful reference examples of different kinds of images, including maps, infographics, photographs, and PowerPoint slides. Each example includes a formula for creating a citation, multiple examples of formatted references, and multiple examples of both parenthetical and narrative citations.[1] There's also a section entitled "Online Media," which also details how to format a reference for materials found online. This section goes into detail on how to create citations for all of the major social media outlets.[2] This is very helpful for students trying to figure out how to create a citation for an Instagram image, for example. There are enough examples in this chapter that the biggest issue that students may encounter with APA image citations is figuring out *which* format is most applicable to their image.

Students may get confused by the differentiation between the different types of image citations here. As a librarian, you may need to help students figure out which of the Visual Works examples is most applicable to the image the student is trying to cite. Some questions your students might have are:

- Is this image from ARTstor a photograph or an artwork in a museum? ARTstor (and other image databases) will include any museum information, if available, which can help students figure out which example to follow.
- Should I cite this as a photograph or as a stock image? For this, students may need to analyze their image source, as well as the content of the image and how they're using it.
- This image was on Twitter *and* on a news website. Which format should I use to cite it? Students would need to think about which image they're *actually* using. Are they just using the image or also the tweet accompanying the image?

Chicago Style

In the 17th edition of the *Chicago Manual of Style*, you'll find plenty of information on how to create many different kinds of citations. In Chapter 14, which details how to create source citations for the notes-bibliography variant of the style, you'll find detailed information on specific kinds of sources, as well as any special cases or examples that the citer might run across. The "Books" section, for example, demonstrates how to cite books who have an editor as well as an author, a single volume in a multivolume work, microform editions, and device-specific e-books, among many others. All of this kind of information is necessary, because so many different kinds of information are associated with books, and there are so many different kinds of special circumstances to consider. The *Chicago Manual of Style* takes the same care with other kinds of sources, including periodicals, websites, and reference works.

However, there is no specific section for citing an image in this chapter. A student looking for the citation rules for images may get stumped here, since they're not listed specifically among the rest of the citation information. They have two options for image citation here: they could utilize the information in the "Audiovisual Recordings and Other Multimedia" section, or they could use the information in Chapter 3, Illustrations and Tables.

Neither choice is a perfect fit for a student needing clarification. The "Audiovisual Recordings and Other Multimedia" section doesn't contain a perfect citation "formula" for digital images. They could adapt the information found in the "Elements of the Citation" section, but they might get confused by the language listed on this page. The medium or format information only lists examples that are applicable to video and audio recording, like MP3 and DVD.[3]

"Illustrations and Tables" offers some additional information on how to properly document images in Chicago style. Again, this section is not a perfect fit for students trying to cite images in this style. For one thing, it's not located in Part III of the Chicago Manual of Style, which is entitled "Source Citations and Indexes," and would be the natural starting point for someone looking for image citation information. Students may overlook Part I, "The Publishing Process," as they're not thinking about *publishing*, they're thinking about *citing*. This section differentiates between captions and credit lines, and students who are unfamiliar with this terminology may not be able to decide which of the two is most appropriate for their usage.

As a librarian, you may find yourself needing to spend extra time with students who are trying to create proper image citations in this style. It's helpful to provide examples and point out the specific rules they need to follow. For example, if you have students utilize the information found in the "Audiovisual Recordings and Other Multimedia" section, then you should take care to provide examples for each element that could apply to images.

MLA Style

The eighth edition of the *MLA Handbook* details the intricacies of the Modern Language Association's publication, writing, and reference style. The *MLA Handbook* doesn't have a listing of examples in one single chapter, where different formulas for different kinds of sources are listed. Instead, there's a section in Part I, "The Principles of MLA Style," that discusses how to create documentation in MLA style.

Within this section, the "Core Elements" subsection lists the common elements that a citation should contain: author, title of source, title of container, other contributors, version number, publisher, publication date, and location.[4] The handbook then goes into detail on how to document each of the common elements, depending on what kind of source each citation is documenting. For location, for example, the handbook describes a number of common ways to document a work's location. A print source's location within a book or article is the page number, whereas the location of an online work is its URL, or web address.[5] However, there are very few examples of images in the *MLA Handbook*, and without these examples, it can be hard for students to figure out exactly how to format their image citations.

One of the best ways that you, as a librarian, can help students attempting to cite images in MLA style is by providing the clear examples that the handbook itself lacks. Most of the information needed to properly format image citations can be found within the handbook itself, but it's very difficult to piece it all together as a student. Providing a handout or webpage that details common image citation issues can go a long way in making this citation style more accessible for your students. See Appendix A for an example of a handout.

Attribution

Attribution refers to when students need to cite images but they do *not* need to use a specific style. Because image attribution doesn't utilize a specific style, these are often much easier to create. The student just needs to locate the metadata about the image instead of finding that metadata and trying to figure out how to plug that into a citation formula.

There are some best practices for creating an image attribution. According to Creative Commons, attributions need to include four things: a title, the name of the creator, the source of the image, and any copyright information.[6] These four pieces of metadata can create a fairly complete idea of what the image is and where it comes from, and it works well when using digital images. For students, image attributions need to include enough information about the image so that other people can evaluate it. Therefore, a student may need to include some more information in their attributions, such as the date or a description.

The beauty of image attribution is that it's flexible. Different kinds of projects and presentations might have differently formatted attributions based on the stylistic limitations of the medium. For example, if a student is creating an attribution on an image they're using on a website or in a blog post, they can feel free to include as much information as they want. The page can be as long as it needs to be; there's no space that's truly limiting students' ability to create an attribution. If someone is creating a citation in a Power-Point presentation, however, there might be room on the slide for as detailed of an attribution as in the other situation. A slide with an illustrative image, for example, may just have a title and a link to the source. A slide with a photograph may just have the title, source, and date. The key is to think about what you need to include in order for the viewer to have enough context to understand the image more fully. An illustrative slide of a clipart image of a map does not require as much context as a photograph of a politician who's been in the news lately.

PHOTO 5.2. [Haircutting in Front of General Store and Post Office on Marcella Plantation, Mileston, Mississippi] by Marion Post Wolcott, 1939. Public domain image courtesy of the Metropolitan Museum of Art.
Source: Courtesy of the Metropolitan Museum of Art.

Let's look at our example image again. Photo 5.2 is the same image, from the same source, as Photo 5.1. However, instead of following the rules and formatting for a proper citation, it simply has an attribution. It contains much of the same information as the original citation, but has a more fluid format.

As always, the best way for students to learn about a topic is to have them actually work with the content themselves. If you're looking for an active, engaging activity on image documentation, be sure to check out Chapter 6's Meme Caption Activity. This activity can be used for either citation or attribution, depending on what your needs are.

LEGAL ISSUES AND IMAGE USE

In addition to documenting images properly, students must have some awareness of image copyright. Image copyright isn't something a lot of people think about. People across the internet have a tendency to use whatever images they find for whatever purpose they'd like, due in part to the share and repost features on many social media websites. The truth, however, is that not all images are free to use for all purposes.

When discussing image copyright, I try to make students understand how important copyright is by appealing to their own sense of ownership. I often ask students if they are creators themselves. Lots of people are creators, even if they don't call themselves that. Do you take pictures, make videos, write songs or stories? How would you feel if someone started using your creations without asking you? What if someone started making money off of your work? This will usually illicit a response and let them begin to empathize with the owners of images.

The depth to which you go into the details depends on your students and why they're using an image. Some kinds of students will need more in-depth image copyright assistance than others. Students who may be trying to publish, such as a graduate student or an undergraduate researcher, will certainly need some more specialized assistance. Second, consider why someone is using an image. Some image-use situations are more complicated than others. In short, if someone just wants to use an image in a classroom setting, that's a simple scenario that's easy to handle with fair use. The more people who see the image, however, the more complicated it gets. Publishing your image to the internet or in a university publication, presenting it at a symposium, or creating a logo or website for a business are all more complicated scenarios that will involve some research and thought.

If you need to help students find images that they can use, there are three main concepts to consider: fair use, Creative Commons, and the public domain.

Fair Use

As a librarian and an instructor, you may have heard of the term "fair use" before. Fair use basically means that certain kinds of information uses are permitted by copyright-restricted resources. Normally people think of documents, like books and articles, in regard to fair use, but it also covers images. Section 107 of the Copyright Act defines fair use and outlines the characteristics that are used to judge whether or not something should be considered fair use.

Fair use is not always easy to determine; you and your students need to make a judgement call for each time you want to use copyrighted materials. To determine whether or not your or your student's use of an image is considered fair use, you need to consider four factors:

- Purpose: What are you using the image for? Is this for a commercial or noncommercial purpose?
- Nature: What is the nature of the work that you're considering using? Is it published or unpublished?
- Amount: How much of the work are you using? Keep in mind that both the quantity and quality of the amount you're using should be evaluated.[7]
- Effect: What kind of effect will your use of this resource have upon the original resource?

Fair use applies to most educational purposes, including using in the class-room for presentations. Be careful if your student wants to publish an image that they find, whether it's online or in print, and even if it's for an educational purpose. Some websites have created and published fair use calculators that you can use to help determine whether or not something could be considered fair use. Just keep in mind that these resources are simply guides and are not offering legal advice.

Creative Commons Licenses

While browsing the internet, you may have noticed some letters in an image attribution or on a website that start with "CC." Perhaps it was an image with a credit that stated CC-BY-ND, for example. You may have found a website or document with a small gray and black image that stated CC-BY-NC. These both mean that resource has a Creative Commons license.

Creative Commons is an organization that works to simplify copyright on the internet by providing different kinds of licenses that creators can attach to their works. According to the Creative Commons organization, these licenses endeavor to help the viewer of copyrighted materials answer the question: *"what can I do with this work?"*[8] Creative Commons licenses range from the very permissive, even allowing for commercial use, to much more restrictive. One thing that all Creative Commons licenses have in common is that they all require that anyone who uses the item must give credit to the original creator.

Creative Commons licenses let viewers know what people can do with their works: whether or not users are allowed to adapt their work, how to license adaptations of the original work, and/or whether or not someone can use it commercially. Adaptation means whether or not users can edit the original product. Some licenses allow for this, while others state that the image or resource cannot be edited or remixed and can only be shared and used in its original form.

There are six different Creative Commons licenses:

- CC-BY licenses are the most permissible. People can do anything with the resource, including use it for a commercial project and edit it, as long as they credit the creator.
- CC-BY-SA licenses are also pretty permissible. People can do anything they want with the resource, including use it for a commercial project and edit it, as long as they credit the creator. If they make an adaptation of the resource, they must share it under the same terms.
- CC-BY-NC licenses do not allow other people to use the resource for a commercial project. So, people can use and edit the resource as long as they credit the creator and use it for a noncommercial project.
- CC-BY-NC-SA licenses also do not allow other people to use the resource for a commercial project. So, people can use and edit the resource as long as they credit the creator and use it for a noncommercial project. If they make an adaptation of the resource, they must share it under the same terms.
- CC-BY-ND licenses do not allow people to edit or adapt the original resource. People can use and share the resource, even for commercial projects, as long as they credit the original creator.
- CC-BY-NC-ND are the most restrictive licenses. People cannot edit or adapt the original resource or use it commercially. People can use and share the resource as long as they credit the original creator.

If a student encounters an image they'd like to use and it has a Creative Commons license, they can easily figure out what kinds of uses are permissible. Likewise, if a student creates an original work, they can use a Creative Commons license to let other viewers know how they can use their work.

Public Domain

Some images are considered to be in the public domain. This means that they are not protected by copyright and other intellectual property laws. Generally, you can use images in the public domain for any purpose, including editing it and publishing it in a commercial publication. Public domain images are a good choice for students who don't want to or who can't license images for their commercial projects or publications.

It's not always easy to determine which images are in the public domain and which ones aren't, however. Knowing a little bit about why certain works enter the public domain can help you and your students determine whether or not something is public domain. Images will fall into the public domain for one of four reasons:

- The copyright has expired. Copyright laws don't protect works of a certain age. You can look up the public domain cutoff year to figure out how old something has to be before it enters the public domain.
- The owner of the copyright has not renewed the copyright. If the owner fails to renew the copyright on their work, it can sometimes be considered within the public domain.
- The owner of the copyright dedicated the image to the public domain. Sometimes, a creator can choose to immediately place their image (or other creation) directly into the public domain.
- It's not a work that can be protected by copyright law. Most notably for images, this includes works created by the U.S. government.[9]

The most effective way of determining if an image is public domain or not is by examining the information on the website on which it was found. If the source has a lot of well-documented metadata about the image, it may also include some copyright information. In these cases, it will usually specify whether or not the image is in the public domain. If not, it will sometimes supply who holds the copyright. This is where using library databases, museum websites, and other image sources you may not encounter right away in Google Image Search results has some real value that students may see.

Need to talk about image copyright? The Wikipedia Pic-a-Thon is a workshop that not only gets students thinking about copyright but also lets them participate by contributing to the public domain. Go to Chapter 6 to find out more about this fun workshop.

Just as students best develop skills and knowledge through use, so do librarians. As you become more familiar with image citations and ethics, you'll become more confident in assisting students and faculty. However, it's important to continually develop your knowledge in these areas. Image copyright and legal issues associated with image use is an ever-evolving topic. Citation styles update, and new legal precedents inform future best practices. Keeping up with updates from style publishers as well as literature about image use will ensure you have the most current information on these topics.

NOTES

1. American Psychological Association. *Publication Manual of the American Psychological Association*. Washington, DC: American Psychological Association, 2020.
2. American Psychological Association. *Publication Manual of the American Psychological Association*. Washington, DC: American Psychological Association, 2020.

3. University of Chicago Press. *The Chicago Manual of Style*. Chicago: University of Chicago Press, 2017.
4. Gibaldi, Joseph. *MLA Handbook for Writers of Research Papers*. New York: Modern Language Association of America, 2015.
5. Gibaldi, Joseph. *MLA Handbook for Writers of Research Papers*. New York: Modern Language Association of America, 2015.
6. Creative Commons. "How to Give Attribution." https://creativecommons .org/use-remix/attribution.
7. U.S. Copyright Office. "More Information on Fair Use." https://www .copyright.gov/fair-use/more-info.html.
8. Creative Commons. "About CC Licenses." https://creativecommons .org/about/cclicenses.
9. Stanford Copyright and Fair Use Center. "Welcome to the Public Domain," April 3, 2013. https://fairuse.stanford.edu/overview/public -domain/welcome.

6

Activities and Assignments

There are a lot of different ways you can start to add more visual literacy instruction to your classes. Database demonstrations and library orientations are both useful tools in instruction, but they don't adequately cover a multifaceted topic like visual literacy. Active learning, where students get to participate in instruction, makes for more engaged students and can also help the lesson stick. If you want to integrate some visual literacy instruction into your curriculum, these activities can help you get started.

Each of these assignments, activities, and workshops can be conducted in a 100% online environment, and many use a variety of different digital humanities tools. There's also additional in-person adaptation information, allowing you to conduct all of these activities in a face-to-face environment just as effectively. Each activity can also be used in a variety of disciplines. Some suggestions can be found for each activity under "Adapting This Activity for the Disciplines."

WAKELET DIGITAL CURATION

There's a lot more to the process of searching for images than simply typing keywords into a search engine. The Wakelet Digital Curation activity allows students to practice all the different parts of the image search, from articulating their image need, to searching for images, to organizing them for ease of use later on. This asynchronous online activity works best when paired with an image-based assignment, but it can also function on its own.

For more information on searching for images, please turn to Chapter 2.

Preparation

- Familiarity with **Wakelet**. Wakelet is a free and easy-to-use web application used for curating collections of digital objects. In this activity, it's used to save and collect digital images. While use of Wakelet is fairly intuitive, you may need to provide some support or a demonstration for students in this activity.

- Optional: **some faculty collaboration**. This activity works particularly well when paired with an image-heavy research project, like a presentation.

Activity Walk-Through

In this activity, students will be using a digital tool called Wakelet to create an informal visual bibliography. This activity really shines when used in conjunction with an image-heavy research assignment. If students need to find several images for a presentation, a poster project, a website, or even a paper, this is a great way to get students practicing finding and organizing images. If students just need general practice in the image search process, you can give them some sort of prompt. Some prompt ideas can be found in the "Adapting This Activity for the Disciplines" section.

First, you need to introduce the concept of image searching to students, stressing that the process of finding images has three distinct stages: articulating your image need, searching for images in databases and on the Web, and finally, organizing found images and metadata for later use. Most people go straight to stage 2—searching—before properly articulating their image needs. It's also helpful to introduce students to the basics of Wakelet. You can introduce these concepts through a short video, or even just a typed document with a link to a sample collection, some sample images, and possibly screenshots of search results. You might find it helpful to share some recommended image resources here, especially if you want students to utilize image databases, rather than simply defaulting to Google Image Search.

After introducing these concepts to students, it's time to have them begin their own three-part image search. First, they need to articulate their image needs. Instruct students to write a brief description of their image needs. It's helpful to offer guidance here. Have them specify what images they're looking for, some possible places they might begin searching, and how they'll use the images. This description should ultimately help students brainstorm some initial keywords. Here are some sample descriptions that articulate a variety of image needs:

- I'm looking for images of women in healthcare. This could be images of women as doctors, nurses, therapists, or other healthcare provider roles. I'm interested to see how women have been portrayed as healthcare workers and how that portrayal has changed throughout time. I plan to start looking for historic images of women healthcare workers, maybe Red Cross nurses from World War II. Then, I want to find some progressively more modern images. I'm going to try to find some contemporary images from hospital websites. I hope to use some of these images in my presentation, so they need to be large and suitable for use in PowerPoint.

- I'm looking for advertisements of different kinds of products from the 1960s. I want to find a variety of different kinds of advertisements, particularly of products that were aimed at different kinds of people. I'm going to start by looking for car advertisements, which were probably created for men. Then, I'm going to look for household cleaning products, which were likely to have been created for women. I'm going to start by looking on some of the museum websites shared by the librarian, and I'm also going to try Google Image Search. I plan on using these images in my paper, so they should be high enough resolution for printing.

Then, students should create a Wakelet account. The accounts are free and don't necessarily need to be tied to a social media account. Students will use Wakelet as a way to digitally organize images, to preserve source information and metadata along with the image itself, and to easily share with instructors and fellow students. Once the student has created a Wakelet account, they can then create a new collection. Students should copy and paste their written image needs into the description section of the collection. The students might need some guidance with the title. Remember, these collections will be shared, so the title should be descriptive and helpful—a title like *Images of Working Women in the 18th Century* is more useful for sharing than a title like *Collection for HIS 1500*, for example. Now, students are ready to begin searching for images, using their description to guide their way.

You should allow time for students to search for images on their own. You should consider making yourself available should a student have difficulty finding images on their own. You could set up a drop-in image search consultation time, for example. Students should find a predetermined number of images and add them to their collections. Images can be added to a Wakelet collection either manually, by clicking on the plus sign while editing the collection, or by using the free browser add-on.

When adding an image to a collection, Wakelet offers users a chance to also add a description and/or caption. While both are considered optional by Wakelet, they are an essential part of this activity. For the credit, students should include information they need to formulate an attribution or citation. You and the instructor can define this caption however works best for your situation. It's easiest to include a link to the source from which the image came, particularly if some or all of the images are going to be used in a later assignment. That way, students have access to the source, which should have the metadata needed for documentation, but students don't have to focus on multiple aspects of visual literacy at a time. Image searching and image citation are both complicated subjects and can be as hard or harder to grasp than traditional document searches and citation.

You have several options of how to handle the final, completed collection of images. If the faculty instructor is amenable, it could be turned in for credit. Simply set the collection's visibility as public or unlisted and then get the collection's URL by clicking on the "share" button when viewing the collection. Students could also present their collections asynchronously on the course page discussion board.

You could also have each student create a discussion board post that links to their collection and provides a short description of what their topic is. In order to do this, you would also need the cooperation of the faculty member. You could offer some direction here by having students answer some prompts like:

- What image source, such as ARTStor, Flickr, or even Google Image Search, did you find the most helpful?
- What kinds of keywords did you use to search for these images?
- What images were you searching for?
- How did your search change over time?

Having students answer questions like that allows them to really dissect and analyze the image search process they just engaged in too. That way, students get practice searching and get a chance to reflect on their image search, so that they may do an even more effective job next time they need images.

In-Person Adaptation

This research project can be conducted just as easily in a virtual or face-to-face environment. Little adaptation is needed for face-to-face classes. However, due to the digital nature of the assignment, you should make sure that students have access to computers in whatever classroom you use. This might mean meeting in a computer lab instead of their typical classroom, or this could mean asking students to bring their laptops to class that day.

This activity is also designed with an asynchronous class setting in mind. The activity requires plenty of individual search time, which doesn't suit every classroom setting. If you're the kind of instructor who prefers not to allot individual search time in the classroom, you can turn this into a group searching activity. Instead of instructing students to create their own board, have them do so in a small group of about four people. Simplify it for the sake of time: have them search for 1 to 3 images instead of 10 or more. Give them a prompt to help spark their image need description, and provide assistance to the groups as they search for their images.

Adapting This Activity for the Disciplines

You can easily use this activity in a variety of specialized disciplines, simply by adapting the initial image search prompt. Here are some ideas for inspiration:

- This works well for any **sociology** class. Students can find images of people of different races, genders, or other demographic factors, and have them find examples that show how these different kinds of people are portrayed in images.
- This is also a great activity for any class that will require lots of image search skills, such as an **art history** course. Students looking to write a paper or complete a project on a topic can use this activity to research for their assignment and practice the image search skills they'll need for the rest of the class.

RGIS SCAVENGER HUNT

The Reverse Google Image Search Scavenger Hunt, or RGIS Scavenger Hunt, prepares students to become image skeptics. There are so many different images and image sources today. As people share and report images, they become increasingly difficult to effectively evaluate, because they're often separated from their image metadata. This activity asks students to track down some missing metadata using Reverse Google Image Search. This is a synchronous class activity that can be utilized in any course that requires students to use digital images.

For more information on evaluating digital images, please turn to Chapter 3.

Preparation

- A selection of sample **images** for your students to evaluate. You'll need one image for each small group in your class. Extra care should be taken in selecting these sample images. They should be images that have been reposted and shared by many different sources, with at least one reliable source somewhere in the first page or so of results.

• Access to an **online video conferencing environment** with the capability to break the class up into smaller groups. Zoom, for example, has breakout rooms.

Activity Walk-Through

First, you'll need to introduce students to the importance of image metadata, how reposting can often separate images from their original metadata, and how we can search for some of that metadata. I like to include an example image that I evaluate for the students so that they can see for themselves. You can introduce these concepts through a short video, or even just a typed document with an example image. This can take place before the class session begins, if you'd like to utilize a flipped classroom style activity, or you can deliver a brief, introductory lecture to the group.

Next, you need to divide students into small groups and send them into breakout rooms. Each group is given a different digital image out of its original context; practically, this means you would send each group an image file, like a .jpg, instead of a link to wherever you found the image hosted digitally. Instruct students to utilize Reverse Google Images Search in order to find a source for their image. Once they've found a source, they need to attempt to find as much metadata about the image as they possibly can. You might find it helpful to give them certain fields to look for: title, creator, date, original source, and/or description, for example. A group could look for information on at least two of those fields. Not all images will have all of those metadata fields—some images don't have titles, for example. In addition, not all groups will likely be able to find the image's original source. The key is teaching them to be critical and flexible in their reverse search skills.

Once all the groups have had sufficient time to search, bring all the students back into the main room of the video conferencing software. Have the groups present their images, and discuss what metadata they were able to find about their image and where that metadata came from. If desired (and if time allows), you can also integrate some image evaluation at this point. Students could make a judgement call on their image's metadata. They could decide whether or not they have enough information to actually use this image in an academic project.

In-Person Adaptation

This activity easily adapts to a face-to-face environment. Instead of utilizing the video conferencing software, simply divide up students into small groups in the classroom. However, due to the digital nature of the assignment, you should make sure that students have access to computers in whatever class-room you use. This might mean meeting in a computer lab, or this could mean asking students to bring their laptops to class that day.

Adapting This Activity for the Disciplines

Changing up the image prompts allows you to customize this activity for a wide variety of classes. Here are some ideas for inspiration:

- This is especially useful in any course that asks students to take a critical look at what they encounter on **social media**, such as a journalism, media studies, or political science course. Assign each group an image from social media that they must track down to its original source.

- This could also be a helpful tool for a course that tackles the issue of **science in the media**. Images that are shared without metadata can be used for purposes that the creator, no matter how reliable, did not intend. Medical images, graphs, and other scientific images are no exception.

- This is also a good activity for any **history** course that wants students to take a critical look at how images are used and shared to perpetuate certain historic narratives. Historic images are often shared without any metadata.

ORCAS CHECKLIST GROUP ACTIVITY

The ORCAS Checklist gives students a set of tools that they can use to **evaluate images**. The ORCAS activity is a synchronous online library session that uses the ORCAS approach to evaluate images from markers of credibility. This group activity is an easy and engaging way to get students thinking about evaluating all the digital images they see. This is a nondiscipline-specific class that's helpful for any course involving an image-based project.

For more information on image evaluation and ORCAS, please turn to Chapter 3.

Preparation

- A **sample image or images** for your students to evaluate. A smaller class of 12 or so students may only need one sample image to work with. Larger classes will need two to four sample images. The sample images should come from different kinds of sources, if using more than one, so that students have the opportunity to see what images from credible and less credible sources look like.

- Access to an **online video conferencing environment** with the capability to break the class up into smaller groups. Zoom, for example, has breakout rooms.

Activity Walk-Through

First, you'll need to introduce students to the concept of image evaluation. Go through each marker of credibility, as outlined by ORCAS. I like to include an example image that I evaluate for the students so that they can see for themselves. You can introduce these concepts through a short video, or even just a typed document with an example image. This can take place before the class session begins, if you'd like to utilize a flipped classroom style activity.

After students have been introduced to the basics of the concept of image evaluation and the ORCAS test, it's time for a group activity. In this activity, groups of students evaluate the same image by one of the factors of the ORCAS test. First, introduce the students to the sample image being used for the class. Include where you found it: if it's from a news site, share the entire website, for example. Try not to separate the image from its context, because students will need that context in order to make their judgement calls. Frame the image as a possible source for a sample research topic. Then, divide the class up into five groups: one group for each factor of ORCAS. Send each group into the breakout room, and have them evaluate the image for their chosen factor of credibility. It's helpful to give them some questions to spark discussion on their factor. They can be simple: Do you think this is an original image? Why? If not, which parts seem to have been reused or modified? Have every group make a judgement call on whether or not they think the image is original, relevant, current or timely, authoritative, and contains the right subject matter.

If your class is particularly large and there are too many students to have just five groups, you can also use more than one image. As mentioned previously, this can be a good way to show the difference between a fairly credible and a noncredible image.

After a few minutes, bring everyone back into the main room. Now, it's time for each group to present their findings. Have a representative from each group make a brief presentation on their group's thought process and their ultimate judgement call on their factor. After each group has presented, have the class as a whole decide on whether or not the image is suitable for the purpose.

In-Person Adaptation

This activity easily adapts to a face-to-face environment. Instead of utilizing the video conferencing software, simply divide up students into small groups in the classroom.

Adapting This Activity for the Disciplines

This activity works well for any course where students are required to use images, including a first-year experience or seminar course, if they're working on a paper, project, or presentation that uses images. Changing up the sample images allows you to customize this activity for a wide variety of classes. Here are some ideas for inspiration:

- This is a great activity for a **journalism** course. You could frame the topic as a possible news story and have students evaluate internet images for suitability for inclusion in the article.
- **History** classes may find this to be a helpful exercise. While it's easy to find images from a variety of historic periods, not all of them are appropriate for use in an academic presentation. It's easy to trick viewers with images with similar subject matter, too.
- This would be a particularly great activity for any course that discusses **social media**. Have students investigate images that come from social media sources. You could frame this activity as: What should you share/repost?

NEWS IMAGE ANALYSIS DISCUSSION POSTS

The News Image Analysis Discussion Posts activity is an asynchronous online library session that gets students thinking about how to **interpret images** they find by using images from news articles as examples. This activity will get students thinking about how images add to narratives and how image vocabulary can be used to make a viewer feel a certain way about the subject of an image. This lesson is perfect for any class that works with the news or popular topics.

For more information on image interpretation, check out Chapter 3.

Preparation

- **Example images** from news sources. You'll need to gather about five to seven images, depending on class size. These images should come from news websites. I've found *The New York Times* to be a reliable source of interesting and easily interpretable images for this kind of activity.

- **Access to the course's page on your learning management system (LMS).** Most major LMSs, like Blackboard or Canvas, will have some sort of discussion posts feature.
- **Cooperation from the course instructor.** Make sure you have the ability to add discussion posts to the course. This usually means you will have to be added to the course in some role—whether that's as an instructor, a teaching assistant (TA), or whatever else works with your community.

Activity Walk-Through

First, you'll need to introduce students to the concept of image interpretation. Discuss how images can be used to make the viewer feel a certain way about what they portray, and show the basic image vocabulary you'll have them use in class. I like to include an example image that I interpret for the students so that they can see for themselves. You can introduce these concepts through a short video, or even just a typed document with an example image.

Then, you'll need to build a series of discussion board posts on the course's page. Include one image per post, and ask students to comment on at least one post, asking them to interpret the image. Prompt them with questions like: How does this image use line, color, or space? How do you feel about the subject of this image? Why would someone choose this image to represent this subject?

Be sure to follow up on the posts, responding to comments in order to jumpstart a conversation. After some posts, you can include the image's source information and see how that changes—or adds to—anyone's image interpretation.

In-Person Adaptation

This activity works equally well in a face-to-face environment. Instead of having students comment on discussion board posts, you can utilize a small-group approach. You'll need to prepare some preprinted images and maybe provide some pens, pencils, or other writing implements.

You start with introducing the concept of image interpretation. You can accomplish this in person through a lecture, or you can utilize a flipped classroom approach by having students watch a prepared video or complete a tutorial on image interpretation. Then, for the activity, you can break students up into small groups of three to five, depending on class size. Present each group with a prepared, printed-out image from a news source. Let students draw on the image in order to see how the photographer has chosen line and space. Students will need to take notes on how the parts of the image affect their viewing of it.

After some time, have students present their interpretations. To accompany the presentation, you can pull up the image in PowerPoint or on the source itself, especially if the source adds interesting context to the interpretation.

Adapting This Activity for the Disciplines

Changing up the image prompts allows you to customize this activity for a wide variety of classes. Here are some ideas for inspiration:

- For a **sociology** course, you can use this activity to demonstrate how different news outlets cover different kinds of people. Choose images of a certain kind of person—whether it's by gender, race, nationality, sexuality, or whatever else might be relevant to the course—and have students interpret how different news outlets showcase different kinds of people. This can be a good way to demonstrate bias in image selection.

- For a **history** course, you can use images from historic newspapers. If you don't have access to a historic newspaper database at your institution, you can use the Library of Congress's helpful Chronicling America database.

- For **political science** classes, this activity is a great way to showcase how the media portrays different political parties. You could find images of the same subject from different news sources—the same politician, perhaps, covered by a right-leaning, a moderate, and a left-leaning news source. Ask the students how the political "lean" of the news source may have affected their image choice.

IMAGE COMPARISON WITH JUXTAPOSE JS

Images, just like every other piece of information created by humans, are shaped by the social, historical, and political circumstances that surround them. Interpreting images through these lenses can offer a fresh take on visual information, one that may offer a more complete picture. The Image Comparison with Juxtapose JS activity is an asynchronous activity that gets students thinking about the importance of context in evaluating images. Students pair an initial image, either one of their choosing or one that's been provided to them, with another image that illustrates the circumstances of the first image. Juxtapose JS allows viewers to use a slider to minimize and maximize the two images, making it an ideal tool for illustrating image comparison.

For more information on interpreting images and image context, please turn to Chapter 3.

Preparation

- Some familiarity with **Juxtapose JS**. Juxtapose JS is a free digital humanities tool that's available from Knight Lab.
- **Access to the course's page on your LMS.** Most major LMSs, like Blackboard or Canvas, will have some sort of discussion posts feature.
- **Cooperation from the course instructor.** Make sure you have the ability to add discussion posts to the course. This usually means you will have to be added to the course in some role—whether that's as an instructor, a TA, or whatever else works with your community.
- **Optional: starting images.** Students can either bring an image that they want to use, or you can provide some initial images.

Activity Walk-Through

First, you need to provide some background information on image context and Juxtapose JS. It's helpful to provide example images here. I use an example of an image of a bustling restaurant in my home city of Nashville as the first image, which needs some context. My second image is that of what the restaurant used to be, which is a predominantly Black church in a now highly gentrified area. You can do this introduction in the form of a video, a PowerPoint presentation, a LibGuide, or whatever else works best for you.

Next, you should introduce the assignment. Students start off with one image, either one of their choosing or one that you've provided to them. It's their job to find another image that provides additional information about the first image. Their final product will be a shareable image with a slider, allowing viewers to view the first and second images side by side.

Students will then spend some time on their own, asynchronously, searching for an additional image that can be used to illustrate the first image's surrounding context. Once they've found their second image, they can create the Juxtapose. To create a Juxtapose, students need to simply navigate to Juxtapose JS's website at juxtapose.knightlab.com and add the appropriate information in the appropriate areas. Students add the URL for the first image in the "left image" area, add a title under "label," and an attribution under "credit." They then do the same for the second image in the "right image" area. They can adjust some settings, but they're not necessary. Students can hit "preview" to see how their Juxtapose will look and then hit "publish" in order to share it. There's both a link and an embed code, making it easy to share in an online environment.

After some time has elapsed, students will then post their completed Juxtaposes into their discussion boards. Students should also write a brief narrative about their images and why they chose the second image. The other students should comment on at least one other student's post, responding how the second image has changed their understanding of the first.

In-Person Adaptation

This activity easily adapts to a face-to-face environment. Instead of utilizing the video conferencing software, simply bring students into the classroom. You can transform this activity into a synchronous activity by turning it into a group activity. Provide an image to each group of three to four students and have them search together for a second explanatory image. Instead of presenting on a discussion board, students can present their final Juxtaposes to the class, who can then comment on how the addition of the second image has changed their understanding of the first.

Due to the digital nature of the assignment, you should make sure that students have access to computers in whatever classroom you use. This might mean meeting in a computer lab, or this could mean asking students to bring their laptops to class that day.

Adapting This Activity for the Disciplines

Changing up the image prompts allows you to customize this activity for a wide variety of classes. Here are some ideas for inspiration:

- This would work well in any **environmental science** class. This is a perfect activity for illustrating the effects of climate change or natural disasters. Students can bring in a current location of their choosing and find the image of that location on Google Earth. You can utilize Google Earth's historical data to find an image of the same place at a different time and compare the two.
- This would also be interesting in any course that covers **museum studies** issues, such as certain history, anthropology, or art courses. You could find an example of a museum artifact for the first image and use the second image to illustrate some context about the first image, especially if the artifact was removed from its country of origin.

IMAGE DESIGN STUDIO CRITIQUE

The visually literate student should be able to use images effectively, and that means they need to evaluate their own image use. This activity is based on the traditional art critique and utilizes peer evaluation. This is a synchronous activity that works in conjunction with an image-based assignment. Students bring a completed draft of their image and pair up with a partner or small group via online video conferencing software. The partners or group members then offer their interpretation of the image to the student who created it, allowing them to see what they did right and what they need to improve upon.

For more information on image use self-evaluation, please check out Chapter 4.

Preparation

- A drafted **image-based assignment**. Students will be peer reviewing a project, presentation, or other kind of image use. The students should have a complete and ready-to-evaluate version of their image. This activity works well with the StoryMap Research Project, which is also detailed in this chapter. If you're working with that project, students could evaluate each other's maps while using this project.
- Access to an **online video conferencing** environment with the capability to break the class up into smaller groups. Zoom, for example, has breakout rooms.

Activity Walk-Through

First, introduce the concept of evaluating your own image use. You can do this via a brief discussion before the activity begins, or you can, with the cooperation of the instructor, have students watch a video or other, similar type of asynchronous introduction beforehand if you'd prefer to use a flipped classroom approach. For either method, it's a good idea to provide an example for students. I usually provide an example of a poor image choice in a presentation along with a better image choice.

Then you can introduce the activity to students. Have them think of this as a peer evaluation of their visual works, much like how they sometimes do peer evaluations of their written works. You should provide some guidance to the students before they go into the breakout rooms. Ask them to consider the image's source and metadata. Is it trustworthy and credible? Can you tell what the subject matter of the images is? Does it add something to the overall project or narrative? Do instruct students to offer kind, constructive criticism only. The goal is to improve their images, not to tear down their peers. They should be evaluating for credibility and how it adds to the project narrative, not a sense of taste or aesthetic quality.

Next, you need to break students up into groups. Depending on the size of the class, this could mean pairs of students, or if your class is particularly large, into small groups. While in the breakout rooms, students need to study their partner's image. They can send a URL or other file through the chat for this. After some time has elapsed, each student takes turns offering their thoughts on the images. They should conclude with a judgement call: I think this works for your project, or I think this isn't clear enough, for example. It's helpful, as the instructor, to jump in between each room to offer your assistance. The activity concludes when each student has received feedback and is ready to make any necessary edits to their image projects.

In-Person Adaptation

This research project can be conducted just as easily in a virtual or face-to-face environment. Little adaptation is needed for face-to-face classes; students could simply show up in class, get paired with a partner, and present their works to each other under your and the instructor's guidance.

Adapting This Activity for the Disciplines

This activity is useful for any course that uses images. Here are some ideas for inspiration:

- This would be a great way for students to evaluate **posters**. Posters often involve images, photos, and other elements of design. Are all of these elements working together to tell the right kind of narrative? Do viewers understand what you're trying to say? The design studio critique can help students answer these questions before turning in a final draft.

- Likewise, you could also use this in any class that requires students to create a **presentation**. Students can also ask their peers if the images chosen for the presentation are appropriate for the format.

- This would be a perfect activity for students to evaluate their own **visualizations,** such as any course that works with data or statistics. Visualizations are notoriously easy to manipulate through number choice, space, and color. Peer evaluation can help students see how their intent may have distorted the data and how to tell their story effectively and ethically.

STORYMAP RESEARCH PROJECT

The StoryMap Research Project is a semester-long librarian–faculty collaboration. While this project has been designed with a general first-year writing or first-year seminar/experience class in mind, it could easily be adapted for other types of courses. In this project, students use digital tools, images, and their own research to tell a story about a specific area of geography. This research project also presents opportunities to embed further visual literacy instruction into a course's syllabus.

For more information on image editing tools and working with faculty, please turn to Chapter 4.

Preparation

- The **cooperation of a faculty member**. This is a research project and not just a one-shot library session. The key to success in this project is having a faculty partner who is interested in collaborating on a research paper alternative.
- **A map-making application.** StoryMap JS, a free tool available online from Knight Lab, is what I've worked with on this project before. You should have some level of familiarity with the program before you introduce it to either the students or your faculty collaborator. If you've never worked with any such programs before, StoryMap JS is a web-based application that is both free and very easy to use.
- **Time.** Since this project is a semester-long collaboration, it may take more of your time than other teaching opportunities.

Activity Walk-Through

To start off this activity, you'll need to meet with your faculty collaborator. A faculty member with an interest in the digital humanities or in research paper alternatives could possibly be interested in working with a librarian on this project. Once you find someone who would like to work with a librarian on designing this assignment, you'll need to pitch the basic idea of the assignment.

The basic pitch of the assignment is this: students will use both their research and writing skills to tell the story of a certain geographical place. They could research a specific neighborhood in their city, tracking the changes that occur over time, for example. The students combine their research narrative with a virtual, visual map of that geographic area. StoryMap uses information from Google Maps to place markers on points, which can then be annotated with text, images, and even video. The map's points can be clicked as if it were a PowerPoint presentation. The maps can be shared easily as a link.

You'll need to cover several other items during this initial meeting, including:

- What checkpoints do you think you'll need assistance with? Or in other words: I can come assist you in class with this assignment multiple times during the semester. What do you need? Do you anticipate students needing assistance in finding appropriate images, designing their maps, or properly citing their materials, for example? If so, you can offer additional help in the form of class sessions (like some of the one-shot activities listed in this book) or other materials, such as video demonstrations or LibGuides.

- What are your other responsibilities? It's a good idea to clarify exactly what the instructor would like for you to contribute. Do they need your assistance in creating a rubric or grading, for example? Discussing this beforehand can make for a clearer and easier partnership.

- How can we share the final maps? These maps should be preserved! If your institution has a digital repository, this could be an interesting addition. Otherwise, you could consider sharing on a class website or other platform.

Once you've had a discussion and outlined your responsibilities, you can make a plan of action for the rest of the semester.

In-Person Adaptation

This research project can be conducted just as easily in a virtual or face-to-face environment. Little adaptation is needed for face-to-face classes. However, due to the digital nature of the assignment, you should make sure that students have access to computers in whatever classroom you use. This might mean meeting in a computer lab on some days, or this could mean asking students to bring their laptops to class on any day they work on their maps. Instead of providing a digital space to present their maps, you could simply have students present on a screen or projector and have them talk through each point on the map, explaining its importance and how it relates to their overarching concept.

Adapting This Activity for the Disciplines

Changing up the image prompts allows you to customize this activity for a wide variety of classes. Here are some ideas for inspiration:

- This could be a really interesting research project for an **environmental science** course. Students could research, for example, how climate change has affected different places. Each student could select a national park or other kind of environment, and use Google Earth and historic photos to track how the environment has changed. Their scientific research could seek to tie these changes to climate change.

- This is an obvious choice for any **history** course as well. Students could focus on one particular area of importance in a historical event and research how it may have affected the event. Students could focus on battles during a war, for example, or trading sites during a specific period of time.

MEME CAPTION ACTIVITY

Citation and attribution are difficult concepts for any librarian to tackle in the classroom. This activity is designed to make a difficult lesson more fun for both the students and the library instructor by letting the students work with memes instead of academic images. In this synchronous activity, students find a meme and then create either an attribution or citation for it. Memes are, of course, much harder to document then, say, an image from a database with a lot of metadata, so this activity will have students really thinking about how the rules apply to their chosen image.

For more information on image citation and attribution, please check out Chapter 5.

Preparation

- Access to an **online video conferencing** environment, such as Zoom. It should have the capability to break the class up into smaller groups. Students will need to be able to utilize a chat function and to share their screens with the class.

Activity Walk-Through

First, you need to provide some information on image documentation. Discuss what you're doing (whether it's citing in a particular style or attributing), why it's important, and provide guidelines on how to create appropriate documentation. The "how" is the most important part of this. Provide a "formula" for the citation or attribution and then create an example that uses that formula. It's helpful if the students can continually refer to these examples throughout the activity.

Then, you need to divide the class up into small groups and send them to the breakout rooms. Once in the rooms, instruct each group to find a meme (or other random image of their choosing). You could also have them bring their meme to class, if you want to eliminate time spent searching for images. Students will then be given a certain amount of time to create appropriate documentation for their image. The group should work together to create as accurate of a citation or attribution as they can.

After a few minutes have elapsed, it's time for students to make their pre-sentations. In each presentation, have each group show the image's source as well as their citation. While presenting, offer feedback on the students' citations or attributions. Should they have found a better source for the image? Did they include all the information that they could? Could they have used Reverse Google Image Search to find more and better informa-tion about the image? It's supposed to be a fun activity that gets them think-ing about how to craft documentation, so be sure to offer more advice than criticism.

In-Person Adaptation

This activity works equally well in a face-to-face environment. Simply group students up when they arrive in class. Due to the digital nature of the assign-ment, you should make sure that students have access to computers in what-ever classroom you use. This might mean meeting in a computer lab, or this could mean asking students to bring their laptops to class that day.

Adapting This Activity for the Disciplines

Changing up the image prompts allows you to customize this activity for a wide variety of classes. Here are some ideas for inspiration:

- This is an obvious choice for a **political science** course. Have students use a selection of political memes instead of memes on a variety of topics.
- This is also a great way to demonstrate the value of image databases in an **art or design** class. Instead of using memes, have some students create citations and captions for images found on the open Web, and have some student groups create image citations or captions for images found in an image database. During the presentation portion of the activity, students can speak about their experiences. Was it difficult to find the needed information? Were the students who used databases more likely to be able to form complete citations? There are benefits and drawbacks to using searches and databases, and this might help highlight some of those differences for students.

WIKIPEDIA PIC-A-THON

Talking about copyright is never easy and sometimes is difficult to engage students with. In this asynchronous activity, students learn about image copyright, the importance of public domain resources, and then actually contribute to the public domain, ensuring that more people get to "picture" our world.

For more information on image copyright and the public domain, please check out Chapter 5.

Preparation

- **Cameras.** Students must have access to cameras in order to complete this activity. Smartphone cameras work very well.
- **Familiarity with Wikipedia.** You'll be asking students to contribute to Wikipedia. Wikipedia itself has several resources that introduce people to the basics of editing.
- **Access to the course's page on your LMS.** Most major LMSs, like Blackboard or Canvas, will have some sort of discussion posts feature.
- **Cooperation from the course instructor.** Make sure you have the ability to add discussion posts to the course. This usually means you will have to be added to the course in some role—whether that's as an instructor, a TA, or whatever else works with your community.

Activity Walk-Through

First, introduce the concept of image copyright and the public domain. Also, take the time to highlight some sources of public domain images, including Wikipedia. Explain how sources like these are important, since more people can access and use them. You'll also need to instruct students on how to add images to Wikipedia pages. You can introduce these concepts through a short video, or even just a typed document with some screenshots of Wikipedia.

Then, have each student find a Wikipedia page of a local site without any images. It's helpful to do a bit of research to provide a list of examples. The institution you teach at might be a good place to get started. Is every building or landmark on campus photographed on the Wikipedia article? Have students pick an area to photograph, which they'll then upload to the appropriate Wikipedia article, making sure to include all necessary metadata and to specify that it's in the public domain.

After a certain period of time, perhaps a couple of days to a week, open a discussion thread on the course's page. In that discussion board thread, have each student report back with a link to their image in Wikipedia. They could link to the article as well and discuss their experience taking the image, visiting the site, and how they feel about the public domain.

In-Person Adaptation

This activity requires some rethinking if you'd like to host it in a face-to-face environment. You could host it in the form of a campus workshop, where you ask students to help contribute to the public domain. Instead of requiring them to report back with their contribution, you could provide a list of pages that need images in their local area and ask them to take the time to provide a photograph for Wikipedia next time they're there.

Adapting This Activity for the Disciplines

Changing up the image prompts allows you to customize this activity for a wide variety of classes. Here are some ideas for inspiration:

- This could work well in a **photography** class. Working with a faculty member on this project would allow them to not only teach their students about photography but also provide them an opportunity to use their photography to engage with their local communities.
- This would be really interesting in a **history** class, if your institution is close to any historic sites that aren't very popular. You could work with the historic site to help document it for Wikipedia, for example.

7

Conclusion

Visual literacy hasn't always been a big part of the information literacy conversation—but that shouldn't be the case. Everyone in the higher education environment, from faculty, to librarians, to students, is already using images in their research. Implementing more visual literacy instruction will make everyone more effective researchers.

SUMMING IT UP

Today, most people see, use, and share images through the internet. Though visual literacy has been thought of as an art—a discipline-specific skill set for librarians—this is no longer the case, due in no small part to the ubiquity of images on the internet. Visual literacy is a complex topic, because it is so multifaceted. Visual literacy isn't just about image evaluation or being able to create pictures; it's about every aspect of finding and using images in today's research.

Because visual literacy is complicated, you may think that teaching visual literacy is complicated. This doesn't have to be the case, as this book has shown. One of the most important things to remember when teaching visual literacy is to teach a manageable amount of information. Start off by integrating one aspect of visual literacy into your instruction, rather than trying to tackle the concept of visual literacy as a whole. Figure out what you want to accomplish with your lessons, and figure out which aspect of visual literacy is most closely aligned with that goal.

Another great way to spread the word about the importance of visual literacy is by speaking to your faculty. Does your campus host professional development teaching workshops or have any other resources for faculty looking to improve their teaching skills? This can be a great opportunity to advocate for more visual literacy in the classroom, particularly in disciplines that haven't traditionally featured it.

MOVING FORWARD

Images are already everywhere, and that certainly won't change in the future. As more and more people gain access to the internet and smartphones, more and more images will be published to the Web.

Image technology is already sophisticated. Skillfully edited images—also known as Photoshops—have been a part of the digital landscape for a few years now. This technology will only get more and more advanced as time progresses. Deepfakes—images and visual content that have been manipulated by machine learning and artificial intelligence to create very believable fake content—are not only becoming increasingly common, but the technology in which they're made is becoming increasingly more accessible.[1]

This stresses the importance of image evaluation. As time progresses, it may become even more difficult for the casual observer to detect modified content and identify original images just by looking at the image itself. The ability to locate metadata associated with an image and evaluate both the metadata and the image itself for reliability, authoritativeness, and relevance will become an invaluable skill. Finding quality images from reliable sources will also be a key skill moving forward. Just like how we stress the value of databases and reliable publishers in information literacy, using known, trustworthy sources for image research can help students avoid convincingly manipulated images.

As instructors in higher education, we can also look forward to exciting developments in the world of digital visual literacy. In recent years, librarianship has become much more critical of itself and of information. Images, and visual literacy, are key fields for future #critlib examination. With each passing year, the technology surrounding digital images changes. New image editing applications are created and shared, as are new methods of sharing images and new tools to analyze images. Keeping up with the ever-shifting digital landscape of image usage and tools will be both a fulfilling challenge and an exciting field of future scholarship for years to come.

NOTE

1. Kietzmann, Jan, Linda W. Lee, Ian P. McCarthy, and Tim C. Kietzmann. "Deepfakes: Trick or Treat?" *Business Horizons* 63, no. 2 (March 1, 2020): 135–46. https://doi.org/10.1016/j.bushor.2019.11.006.

Appendix

What If . . .?: Common MLA Citation Questions and Answers

What if I need to cite a digital image in MLA format?

Don't panic! Just follow this format:

Last name, First name. "Title." *Website Title*, Website Creator, Date Created, URL.

What if I'm missing some information?

It's OK if you're missing some information. Find as much information as possible to include in your citation.

What if I have no information?

You can't cite an image if you don't have any information about it. You need to go back to its source—the website you found it from—and see if you can find an artist, title, date, or other information about it. If you can't find anything, you should look for another image to use instead.

What if I need more help?

Your librarian is here to help! *Include your contact information here.*

Index

About the Author

NICOLE M. FOX, MLIS, is an assistant professor and research and instruction librarian at Belmont University, where she teaches instructional library sessions in a variety of undergraduate courses. Fox also serves as the liaison to the School of Design and Department of Art, and she has a BA in art history. She's presented on visual literacy at ACRL. Prior to working at Belmont, Fox was director of information resources at O'More College of Design, where she headed the library and IT departments.